MILITARY VEHICLES

in detail

SdKfz 231/234 8-rad

8 x 8 Armoured Car

MILITARY VEHICLES

in detail

SdKfz 231/234 8-rad

8 x 8 Armoured Car

TERRY J. GANDER

Ian Allan
PUBLISHING

Acknowledgements

This book could not have been produced without
the invaluable assistance of the following people:
David Fletcher, Historian at the Tank Museum *(TM)*,
Bovington, Dorset, England, and the Librarian Janice Tate;
the museum's photographer, Roland Groom *(TM)* for original
images and prints from archive material.
Also thanks to Trans Bus International *(TBI)* for access
to the Dennis archive and to Will Fowler at the Bugle
Archive *(BA)* for World War Two images.

> *Jasper Spencer-Smith*
> Bournemouth, England
> July 2003

Conceived & Edited by Jasper Spencer–Smith.
Design and Illustration: Nigel Pell.
Produced by JSS Publishing Limited,
Bournemouth, Dorset, England.

Title spread: The spoils of war, Allied troops in North Africa examining
a captured sPzSpWg SdKfz 231 8-rad. *(TM)*

First published 2003

ISBN 0 7110 2990 3

Published by Ian Allan Publishing

an imprint of Ian Allan Publishing Ltd, Hersham,
Surrey KT12 4RG.

Printed by Ian Allan Printing Ltd, Hersham,
Surrey KT12 4RG.

Code: 0310/A3

CONTENTS

CHAPTER ONE

DEVELOPMENT

There is an old military axiom which states that 'time spent in reconnaissance is seldom wasted'. Nowhere is this axiom so apposite as when applied to armoured warfare, and the German *Blitzkrieg* in particular.

During the early years of the World War Two, when the *Panzer* divisions reigned supreme, the progress of operations was based around applying the maximum amount of force at the enemy's weakest point. This is an age-old military practice but it always introduces the problem for commanders of where might that weakest point be?

In the old days of traditional warfare, when one line of troops confronted another almost within conversation distance, the strong and weak points of any enemy deployment were almost always apparent to the naked eye of the commanding officers on both sides. As warfare developed during the 19th century and it became possible to organise and control larger and larger bodies of troops, the equally growing power of artillery and the rifled musket meant that battle lines could no longer be concentrated or overseen in the old time-honoured manner. Scouting groups of highly mobile soldiers had to be introduced to find the location of an enemy, how it was deployed and in what strength, reporting back their findings to a higher command level as rapidly as possible.

The scouting function had always been the task of light cavalry, although up to the mid-19th century their role was usually limited to just finding the location of an enemy's main force. By the time of the American Civil War (1861-5) that role had been expanded to include battlefield scouting or reconnaissance and the die was cast for the form that light cavalry operations were to assume from then onwards.

The role of the light cavalry became to move ahead of a main force to determine if the line of advance was clear and report back to higher echelons when contact was made. The reports were meant to contain as much data on the enemy's numbers, intentions and actions as could be derived by observation alone. This had to be accomplished without the enemy knowing their location or objective. There was also the closely associated role of deep penetration raids into an enemy rear to gain intelligence as well as generally harass the enemy, causing as much mayhem as possible by using hit-and-run tactics. In both roles the light cavalry had to do its best to deny the enemy the freedom of action to do the same.

Reconnaissance became a highly specialised military art involving high mobility, guile and sound tactical sense. Light cavalry requirements therefore involved specialised training imparting daring, land navigation, fieldcraft

Above:
An early propaganda illustration of an early *schwererPanzerspäh-wagen* (sPzSpWg) *SonderKraftfarhzeug* (SdKfz 231) 8-rad apparently negotiating an obstacle course during driver training. *(TM)*

Left:
Another propaganda shot of an early production sPzSpWg SdKfz 231 8-rad — note the large and floppy *Panzertruppe* beret worn by the commander in both these photographs. *(TM)*

Above:
Training in the field with an early production sPzSpWg SdKfz 231 8-rad. What appear to be air intakes on the hull front are in fact tool attachment points. *(TM)*

and making maximum use of mobility and concealment. If a reconnaissance or raiding force did make direct contact with an in-force enemy it had to somehow get away as fast as possible as its light strength, limited weaponry and lack of support equipment precluded any serious combat.

These light cavalry tactics still applied when World War One started in 1914. During the great Schlieffen-inspired sweep through Belgium the German Army's massed infantry columns were preceded and screened by *Uhlans* (light cavalry). However, once the main French and British armies made direct contact with the main body of the German forces the time for light cavalry was over. Despite its commanders' continued optimism, there was no place for horse cavalry of any kind during the Western Front trench warfare that continued until 1918. However, German cavalry was used widely on the Russian Front until late 1917.

Light cavalry tactics of a sort did reappear in 1918 although applied to foot soldiers, namely the lead elements of the *Sturmtruppen* (storm troops), the elite assault infantry formations that made the German Spring Offensive so successful during its early stages. Following an intense and concentrated artillery barrage, the main role of these specially trained troops was to infiltrate deep into the Allies' rear areas. Once

there, and using their speed and the mobile firepower they carried with them, they disrupted communications and supply lines, denying the Allies the will and means to fight on as they became increasingly isolated from nearby forces and any form of command structure. The *Sturmtruppen* were extremely successful in all this, especially during the early stages of a succession of major assaults based around them and their tactics. Yet they too had to rely on lead reconnaissance elements to discover and lead the rest of the *Sturmtruppen* units through weak points in the Allied lines and avoid any remaining points of resistance, leaving them for other follow-on units to neutralise.

The *Sturmtruppen* were eventually overcome, not only by Allied counter-measures but also by the fact that they had to proceed on foot. This necessarily limited their mobility and physical endurance so eventually they had to come to a halt, losing the momentum of their attacks. Yet the impact of storm troop tactics was not lost during the period of post-war German staff analysis that was intended to prepare the German Army for its next major conflict.

The next time there would be a change. Following a period of proposals from far-sighted individuals and subsequent lack of encouragement from conservative military decision makers within the German *Reichswehr*

Above:
A good frontal view of an early production sPzSpWg SdKfz 231 8-rad showing detail of the front suspension and equipment locations — note the *Waffen-SS* runes on the registration plate. *(TM)*

9

(and the later *Heereswaffenamt*), there appeared a set of novel tactical concepts broadly built along those drawn up for the *Sturmtruppen*, although with significant innovations. The main change was that *Sturmtruppen* foot soldiers would be replaced by armoured fighting vehicles, the *Panzerwaffe*.

It took time for the new concepts to be accepted and adopted but after the *Nationsozialistische Deutsche Arbeiterpartei* (NSDAP) came to power in 1933 their attractions were enthusiastically embraced by the new political executive, *Panzer* supporters being given every encouragement and assistance. The new *Panzer* divisions were born and with them a whole new array of *Blitzkrieg* tactics with, at their base, a continuation of the *Sturmtruppen* infiltration tactics of 1918. By 1939 the new tactics were ready to be tested in combat, combined with that other novel weapon of war, the aeroplane, to add its particular measure of direct support for ground operations.

Interim

As before, the new tank-based formations needed integrated reconnaissance elements, but with an added importance. For the *Panzers* to have their maximum shock effect they had to strike where the enemy was weakest and where an armoured attack would be least expected. Reconnaissance thus became more important than ever for it took time and effort to concentrate armoured formations and prepare them for an attack. When attacks were to take place *en masse* it became increasingly critical to ensure that the attacks were directed against the correct locations.

In 1933 the German cavalry still retained a large portion of the reconnaissance task. Thereafter they were gradually replaced by mechanised units as it became accepted that horses were too vulnerable to the effects of modern warfare. That is not to say that German horsed cavalry faded away completely, for they did not, some units being still on the active list in 1945. A cavalry division was involved in the invasion of the Netherlands in May 1940, and cavalry units were widely employed behind the lines on the post-1941 Eastern Front, mainly engaged in anti-partisan and similar operations.

They appeared only rarely anywhere near the main combat areas.

It was always intended that the German Army of 1939 would have air observation support and it was duly provided. Reconnaissance aircraft, such as the asymmetric BV141, were developed specifically for the task, although it was appreciated that to rely on airborne observation platforms alone would be ill-advised. In 1939, as in 1918, the weather remained a limiting factor during any air operations while even aeroplanes could not be everywhere at once. When available, air observation was employed for all manner of far-reaching reconnaissance missions, including air-to-ground photography. Airborne findings were often of the greatest importance but were

Above:
Imposing in
appearance but
possessing only
limited tactical
mobility, a sPzSpWg
SdKfz 231 6-rad.

never relied upon completely by any German commander.

Land reconnaissance platforms, once away from the horse, included motorcycles and armoured cars. The motorcycle remained part of German *Aufklärungs* (Reconnaissance) battalions until 1945. Both two-wheel and sidecar models were involved as both were handy, agile and fast. Their main shortcomings were vulnerability, lack of mobility over rough terrain, and exposure to the elements. On the Eastern Front motorcycle operations were often restricted by the weather as much as by enemy actions. In practice, most motorcycle battalions were assigned to motorised infantry regiments within the *Panzer* divisions.

Many of the motorcycle's shortcomings could be overcome by the armoured car, and it was on the armoured car that German commanders came to rely most for forward reconnaissance. When the *Reichswehr* was first formed during 1919 it was not supposed to have any form of armoured vehicle, although limited numbers of armoured cars were permitted for internal security and other policing tasks. Using this concession as a cover, armoured cars also became a clandestine *Reichswehr* asset, although the first armoured cars that were available were hardly of the type that could be employed for reconnaissance.

As they were intended for internal security duties, the German armoured cars of the early

1920s (and for some time after) were armoured juggernauts based on commercial truck chassis. They were high, bulky and bristled with weapon ports but, even with examples provided with a four-wheel-drive (4 x 4) configuration, their weight, thin-rimmed wheels, lack of suspension and general awkwardness, all combined to preclude them from travelling on anything but roads. Once off roads they were virtually immobile so they were hardly suited for military purposes in the field.

These shortcomings were recognised by the issue of a table of performance specifications compiled by *Reichswehr* planners during 1926 and 1927 to satisfy future requirements. In broad terms they called for specialised, lightly armoured reconnaissance vehicles possessing a high degree of all-terrain mobility. Two basic types were requested, light and heavy. The intention was that the bulk of the reconnaissance duties would be carried out by the light model, the heavy model being reserved for long-range reconnaissance missions and generally supporting the light vehicles.

The light requirement was satisfied first. The first result was a conversion of an Adler Standard 6, a 4 x 2 commercial passenger car modified by the addition of armour, a machine gun and other military equipment. The result became the *Kraftfahrzeug 13* (Kfz13 - motor vehicle 13) with a crew of two. The first examples appeared during 1933, although most were built by Daimler-Benz during 1934. From the outset, the Kfz13 was meant to be an interim expedient. It had an open top, limited off-road mobility and no radio. The lack of a radio was not a great drawback as it was intended that the Kfz13 would always be accompanied by a Kfz14, an identical but unarmed vehicle provided with a radio installation.

The Kfz13 had its shortcomings but it remained a valuable training and familiarisation vehicle with which the reconnaissance troops of the early war years could train and formulate tactics. Although officially declared obsolete in 1939, some managed to remain in active service until 1941.

The Kfz13 was replaced by the *Sonderkraftfahrzeug 221* (SdKfz 221 - special purpose vehicle 221) series of light armoured cars that entered service from 1936 onwards and served until 1945, mainly in the form of the more heavily armoured and armed SdKfz 222. As early as 1941 it was considered wanting in

many respects so from 1943 the SdKfz 222 was supplemented by the more mobile SdKfz 250/9 light armoured half-track.

Early 8 x 8s

It was accepted that the 1926-7 lists of specifications for reconnaissance vehicles would preclude the involvement of even extensively modified existing commercial vehicle chassis. As one example, the list of technical specifications included the need for the vehicle to be driven at speed as readily from the rear as from the front, the changeover

in drive mode taking less than ten seconds. In addition, an amphibious capacity for river crossings was requested. These demands placed the required vehicles into a highly specialised category. When joined by other stringent requirements, it became apparent that new designs would have to be developed from scratch.

This was particularly seen with the proposed heavy reconnaissance vehicle, where a multiple-wheel-drive configuration was considered necessary to impart the required level of cross-country mobility. Two possible drive configurations emerged, eight-wheel-drive (8 x 8) and ten-wheel-drive (10 x 10). Test beds (perhaps technology demonstrators

would be a better term) were produced accordingly and tested at the German clandestine testing ground at Kazan, deep in the Soviet Union and away from the scrutiny of Versailles Treaty observers. As an added cover, the test vehicles were referred to as *Mannschaftstransportwagen* (personnel carriers).

Contracts were issued for three test vehicles although it appears that one was not completed. That was the 8 x 8 vehicle contracted to Magirus (Klöchner-Humboldt-Deutz) of Ulm/Donau. Daimler-Benz of Stuttgart-Untertürkheim produced two examples of an 8 x 8 vehicle with all-wheel steering. Büssing-NAG of Braunschweig produced a 10 x 10 vehicle, again with an advanced steering system. Neither of these designs was equipped with turrets or armament, although provisions were made for them to be added at a later stage of testing.

There is no need to go into any great depth with these early prototypes. Although they introduced and tested many novel technical features and sub-systems they both displayed shortcomings of varying importance, most of which could no doubt have been eliminated following further development work. They also showed every sign of being excessively expensive to manufacture and procure in the anticipated quantities. By 1930 the state of the Weimar Republic economy was so precarious that, with no short-term results likely to be forthcoming and with no further development funds in prospect, all work on the prototypes ceased.

More Interims

With the demise of the specialised design prototypes the need for some form of heavy reconnaissance vehicle (*schwerer Panzerspähwagen* - sPzSpWg - heavy armoured reconnaissance vehicle) still existed and had to be met somehow. The German military authorities therefore re-issued their 1926-7 specifications but this time in an amended form as the end product would necessarily have to be based on existing commercial truck chassis since nothing more suitable could be contrived within the required time scale. One result was that the amphibious requirement was eliminated. Once again, the requested vehicles were intended as interim expedients only until something better became available.

Eventually three manufacturers became involved, the same as for the advanced 1926-7 programme. Each manufacturer produced its own particular six wheel, four-wheel-drive (6 x 4) truck chassis and front-mounted petrol engine installation as a basis. The three manufacturers were, once again, Daimler-Benz (G-3a truck), Büssing-NAG (G-31 truck) and Magirus (M-206 truck). All three produced the chassis for what were externally almost identical vehicles as virtually the same armoured body (manufactured by the Deutsche-Werke AG at Kiel and the Deutsche Edelstahlwerke at Hannover) was built onto each manufacturer's

chassis. The armour had a thickness of .32in (8mm) all round.

The result was adequate but not remarkable. The chassis had rigid axles with leaf springs so cross-country performance was limited, especially as it emerged that the vehicles were under-powered. The two-ended driving requirement of the 1926-7 specifications was provided, although all steering was carried using what were the normal front axle wheels only.

The usual crew strength was four.

Most of the type were manufactured in a rather unhurried manner between 1932 and 1936. There were three main models.

sPzSpWg SdKfz 231. This was the main heavy armoured reconnaissance model armed with a small, turret mounting either a single 7.92mm MG13 or MG34 machine gun, or the same gun in a co-axial mounting with a 2cm KwK 30 cannon. An alternative designation was

Waffenwagen (weapon vehicle). Some vehicles had provision for an extra turret-roof-mounted 7.92mm air-defence machine gun.

sPzSpWg (Fu) SdKfz 232. On this model the (Fu) denoted Funk (radio) as it carried a 100-Watt radio installation, its presence indicated by a heavy-frame aerial array supported at its front end over the turret. The SdKfz 232 retained the same armament as the SdKfz 231. An alternative designation was *Funkwagen* (radio vehicle).

Above:
The two forward aerial frame supports over the turret denote this example is a sPzFuWg SdKfz 233 6-rad armoured command vehicle — this example was manufactured by Büssing-NAG.

Above:
An early production sPzSpWg (Fu) SdKfz 232 8-rad, recognisable by its frame aerial array. Note the *Waffen-SS* registration plate. *(TM)*

sPzFuWg SdKfz 263. This was an armoured command vehicle with an extra long-range radio installation, again with a heavy fixed-frame aerial array. The turret was fixed and the armament restricted to a single 7.92mm MG13 or MG34 machine gun. Much of the interior space was occupied by the extra radios and other equipment used for the command role.

The production numbers for the series were limited in comparison to what appeared to have been accepted at the time. Despite reports of totals of about 1,000 vehicles being completed it appears that production of the SdKfz 231 and 232 was limited to 123. A further 28 examples of the SdKfz 263 were manufactured.

Although it was meant to be gradually

Left:
sPzSpWg 231
8-rad on parade
with a sPzSpWg (Fu)
SdKfz 232 8-rad
following. *(TM)*

replaced soon after the last example was
completed during 1936, the SdKfz 231 series
remained in widespread service throughout the
early war years. One of its main contributions to
military proceedings of the time was that it
added its part towards a misleading impression
of German armoured vehicle strengths. This was
accomplished by its frequent appearances on
newsreel and publicity photographs taken

during the German military incursions into
neighbouring states during 1937 and 1938, and
later the 1939 and 1940 campaigns in Poland
and France. After the France 1940 campaign the
SdKfz 231s were withdrawn from front-line
duties to be re-directed for training purposes or
issued as general patrolling and policing vehicles
in occupied territories. Their replacement was
the *Achtrad*, the 8 x 8 armoured car series.

Right:
A good detail view
of a sPzSpWg (Fu)
SdKfz 232 8-rad
complete with a
Pakschütz mounted
on the front for extra
protection. *(TM)*

CHAPTER TWO

GS CHASSIS & ENGINE

While the family of 6 x 4 chassis armoured reconnaissance vehicles might have formed a stopgap until something better became available, during 1933 and 1934 that something still had to be devised.

Once again the German procurement authorities issued a list of specifications along much the same lines as their 1926-7 request but, once again, with the fully amphibious requirement omitted. A wading depth performance of about 3.28ft (1mtr) was substituted. That was during 1934.

That same year the German Army embarked on an ambitious programme to determine what it might expect regarding advanced technology trucks capable of meeting the toughest cross-country and other requirements. One of the outcomes developed under contract by Büssing-NAG at Leipzig-Wahren was an 8 x 8 load-carrying chassis with steering on each of the eight wheels. Much of the technology involved stemmed from the original 1926/7 armoured reconnaissance vehicle specification and the resultant test bed vehicles. The chassis was known (in full) as the *schwerer Einheits Geländegängiger Wehrmachts Lastkraftwagen* (heavy standard cross-country military vehicle).

This chassis was never built for truck purposes. In 1934 the newly forming and expanding German armed forces had many other higher priorities than trucks. Trucks lacked the glamour and propaganda value of armoured

vehicles and aircraft. Once it was realised that the Büssing-NAG 8 x 8 chassis would prove to be a very expensive solution to meet the German Army's future load-carrying requirements, the programme was cancelled, along with several other advanced but lighter truck designs. The old recourse to an interim solution was therefore put into motion yet again. To meet the expanding needs of the German armed forces, existing commercial vehicles were modified to provide some form of relatively modern truck fleet but they were never fully satisfactory for the military role. Nor were the numerous commercial trucks, including captured types, that were later employed in lieu of anything else. The *Wehrmacht* never did obtain the heavy all-terrain truck that could have been so valuable on the post-1941 Eastern Front and elsewhere.

Not to be outdone, Büssing-NAG therefore proposed a modified form of its chassis, known by its design suffix as the GS, to act as basis for the heavy armoured reconnaissance vehicle requirement. The GS chassis, revised to accommodate the requested double-ended steering feature, could assume an armoured hull and all the other necessaries for the reconnaissance role. The German authorities

Above:
Detailed rear view taken by Allied technical staff of a captured sPzSpWg SdKfz 231 8-rad showing a spare wheel stowed and the wire mesh protective shields over the exhaust mufflers. *(TM)*

Left:
Another rear view of a captured (without armament) sPzSpWg SdKfz 231 8-rad with the engine compartment cover opened downwards to provide access to the engine compartment. *(TM)*

agreed so design and development work commenced using the official designation of *Versuchskraftfahrzeug 623 and 624* (experimental vehicle 623 and 624).

It was intended that the new *Achtrad* (8-rad) vehicles would carry out the same roles as those assumed by the 6 x 4 series so, after an interlude from 1937 to 1939 when the designations SdKfz 233 and SdKfz 234 were applied, by some quirk of military designation policy introduced in October 1939, the same SdKfz 231 and SdKfz 232 numbers as before were carried over to the new series. Yet the ordered world of the German logistic infrastructure demanded that some differentiation between the two completely different vehicle types had to be retained, especially as the two would be serving side by side simultaneously for an appreciable length of time. The new vehicles thus became known as the sPzSpWg SdKfz 231 (8-rad), sPzSpWg (Fu) SdKfz 232 (8-rad) and sPzFuWg SdKfz 263 (8-rad). The 6 x 4 vehicles thereafter assumed a 6-rad suffix.

Mechanicals

The production centre for the sPzSpWg SdKfz 231 (8-rad) was the Deutsche Werke at Schichau to where the GS chassis was delivered from Büssing-NAG. The armoured hull, turret and armament were all installed at Schichau. Production commenced during 1936, although initially at a sedate pace, the first example not being delivered to the *Wehrmacht* until 1937.

In 1938 a slightly revised model with some automotive and armour modifications was introduced. For example, the early models were powered by a 7,910cc V-8 Büssing-NAG L8V-GS petrol engine developing 150 to 155hp at 3,000rpm. After 1938 these engines were rebored to enlarge the swept capacity to 8,360cc, increasing the power output to 180hp at 3,000rpm. Maximum road speed was then 53mph (85km/h), or up to 18.6mph (30km/h) off roads.

The GS chassis frame acted as the assembly foundation for the armoured hull and all the automotive components but was still relatively light as the complete bare chassis weighed only 9,083lb (4,120kg). Some engineers considered that the chassis frame was largely redundant as a load-carrying structure as its strength was negligible compared to that imparted by the armoured hull of the vehicle.

Even so, the chassis' main strength was derived from two fore-and-aft, parallel side members with a 'Z' configuration cross section. To simplify manufacture these main members retained a constant depth along their entire length. The two side members were joined together by two tubular main cross members that also acted as the pivots on which the two forward and two rear suspension bogie assembly springs pivoted. Six auxiliary channel-sectioned cross members, each rigidly attached to the main members, provided additional strength and rigidity. The bottom surfaces of the

Fahrgestell Baumuster GS

Z-section main members were used as the location points for components such as the main fuel tank, the gearbox and other items, all so arranged that they could be readily lifted out. In general, maintenance and other access to the vehicle's automotive and associated components was rated as good.

The V-8 Büssing-NAG L8V-GS engine, with its two banks of four cylinders placed at an angle of 90° from each other, was located towards the rear of the chassis frame. As both ends could act as the forward end of the vehicle the exact definition of front and rear remains debatable. Be

that as it may, the engine was located under the longer sloping portion of the armoured hull, with top and side access possible through hatches at the top and sides of the hull. Twin Solex 48 FNVP (later 40 MOVS) carburettors were provided but generally speaking the engine installation was unremarkable, other than the odd side location of the Bosch starter motor. Engines could have either cast-iron or aluminium cylinder blocks, usually the former in view of the critical shortage of bauxite and other raw materials involved with aluminium alloys after 1939. Under desert conditions the air filters

Above:
The basic chassis for the sPzSpWg SdKfz 231 8-rad series photographed from the front as indicated by the rearward sloping steering wheel for the driver. This illustration is from an original *Wehrmacht* service and parts manual.

23

Above:
Another detailed view of the basic chassis for the sPzSpWg SdKfz 231 8-rad series taken from the rear left-hand side. This and most of the other detail component pictures, were taken at the Dennis Works at Guildford, Surrey, England, where two examples of the 8-rad series were taken for detail examination. *(TBI)*

Right:
A sPzSpWg SdKfz 231 8-rad with the rear engine compartment fully exposed after the removal of armour and clearly showing the location of the radiators and cooling fans. *(TBI)*

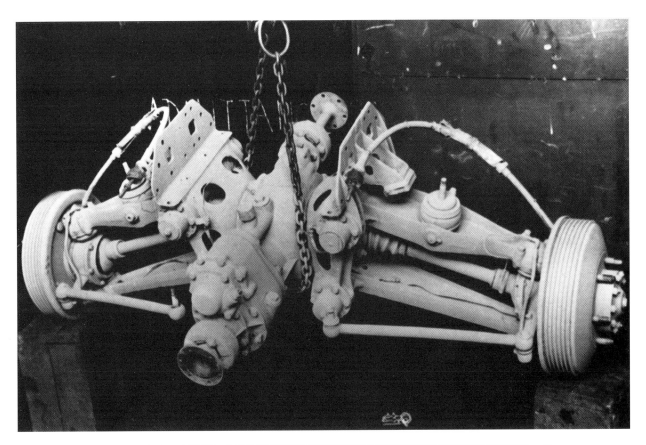

Above:
A sPzSpWg SdKfz 231 8-rad axle and suspension unit removed for detail examination. *(TBI)*

Left:
The steering links, rods and bearings for the rear axle of a sPzSpWg SdKfz 231 8-rad. *(TBI)*

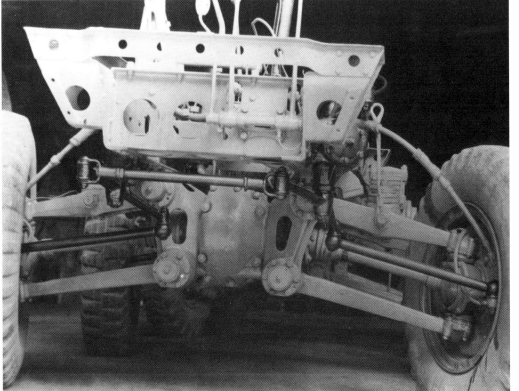

provided proved inadequate, causing excessive cylinder bore and piston ring wear.

For engine cooling, the water-filled radiator was located at the inboard end of the engine, cooling air being drawn through the radiator mesh via hand-adjustable louvres in the hull top plate by two belt-driven fans. Part of the radiator also served to cool the engine oil. Outlet air was passed outside the vehicle through horizontal louvres at the rear of the hull. Experience was to demonstrate that this cooling system was inadequate for operations under hot conditions, especially when the vehicle had to travel towards the rear for long distances.

Drive was taken from the engine by a Fichtel & Sachs or Long twin disc dry clutch and a jointed coupling shaft with Jurid bearings. The gearbox, located in the centre of the vehicle, was of the constant mesh helical gear type with six ratios available, both forward and to the rear. Two levers and a foot pedal, duplicated at each of the two driving stations, were used to select the gears. From the gearbox the drive was taken forward and to the rear, to two double-reduction boxes, each located between the two wheel axles of the front and rear bogie sets. The final drives passed though a Zahnradfabrik Friedrichshafen Aktiengesellschaft (ZF) cam-type differential of the free-wheel type. A De Lavaud type compensating gear was housed in each of the primary sections of the final drive to compensate for the varying drive rates necessary during turns.

The final drive was via the hubs and stub axles. The roller bearings in the hub bearings had to assume considerable loads so were rather prone to wear. The road wheels themselves were of the conventional three-piece, pressed steel type carrying low pressure, cordless 210 x 18 tyres. Each tyre had a self-sealing inner coating for the inner tube. Due to acute shortages of natural rubber throughout German industry the tyres were manufactured using *Buna* synthetic rubber.

For the independent suspension, each of the eight wheels was linked to the chassis frame by two swinging levers, one over and the other below the shaft coupling each road wheel to its final drive gearbox. The upper lever arms were connected in two bogie pairs each side and sprung on a single inverted, semi-elliptic, seven-leaf spring. Once again, the bearings for the swinging lever links had to assume considerable loads so were very prone to premature wear and must have demanded constant checking and maintenance. Maximum vertical wheel movement was 11in (280mm).

Above:
This view of the Büssing-NAG L8V-GS petrol engine clearly shows its compact arrangement. *(TBI)*

Left:
A front-left view of the Büssing-NAG L8V-GS petrol engine as installed in all variants of the sPzSpWg SdKfz 231 8-rad series. *(TBI)*

Right:
Dashboard details
from the original
Wehrmacht manual.
All instruments were
manufactured by
VDO. Note the
speedometers are
marked each side
0-90km/h.

Below:
Also from the same
manual. At the top is
the six-speed gearbox
whilst below is one of
two reduction boxes.
Both units to the left
are fitted with their
ancillary equipments.

To say the worm-and-gear steering system of the *Achtrad* was complicated would be an understatement as a steering wheel, column and gearboxes had to be provided at each end of the vehicle, both stations connected via a system of linking rods and bearings to all eight road wheels. There was no form of powered control, all steering motions being manual although partially assisted by the system gearing. The steering wheel at the usual front end was inverted to save internal space while that at the rear was set at a more orthodox angle. To complicate matters somewhat it had been decided that the front steering wheel would impart more steering leverage that that at the rear. Thanks partially to the De Lavaud compensating gear housed in each of the final drives, during turns it was possible for each of the road wheels to follow the exact track of the one in front. The minimum turning circle diameter was 37.4ft (11.4mtr).

Wheel brakes were cable-operated with Bendix servo assistance.

Two fuel tanks were provided, main and auxiliary. The main tank internal volume was compromised by its rectangular shape having to accommodate numerous grooves to allow the passage of control rods and other shafts. This was mainly caused by the tank location between the two chassis side members. The tank could therefore hold only 24gal (109ltr), so it was backed up by a 6.5gal (29.5ltr) auxiliary tank that fed its contents into the main tank by gravity. The auxiliary tank, being more accessible due to its location in the upper hull, could be used to refill the main tank. One fuel filling could provide an operational range over firm surfaces of about 186.4miles (300km), dependent on terrain conditions and other factors. For cross-country travelling 93.2miles (50km) was a more typical operating range figure.

Bosch manufactured all the electrical equipment for the vehicle, including the starter motor, ignition system and pumps, as it did for many other German armoured vehicles. The electrical circuits could be either 12 or 24V, requiring two 12V batteries.

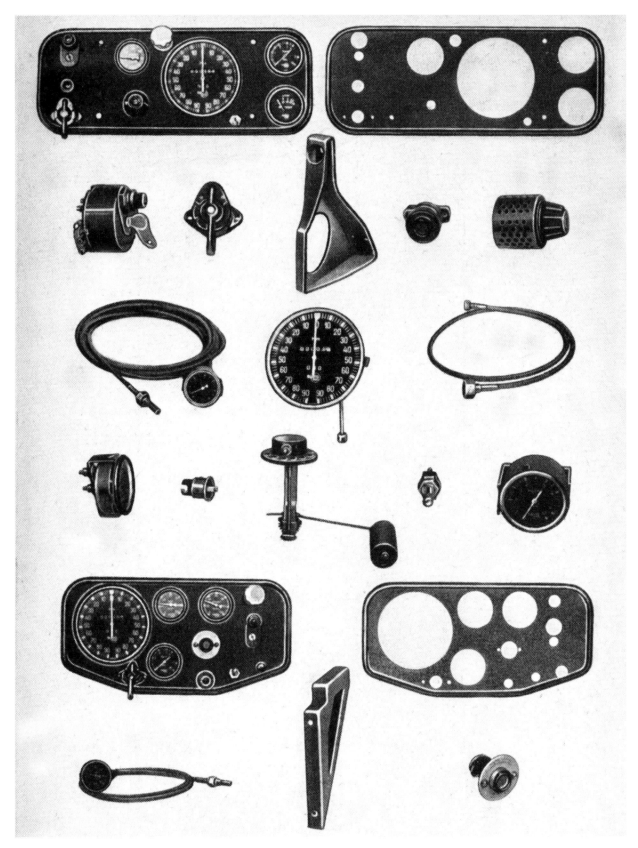

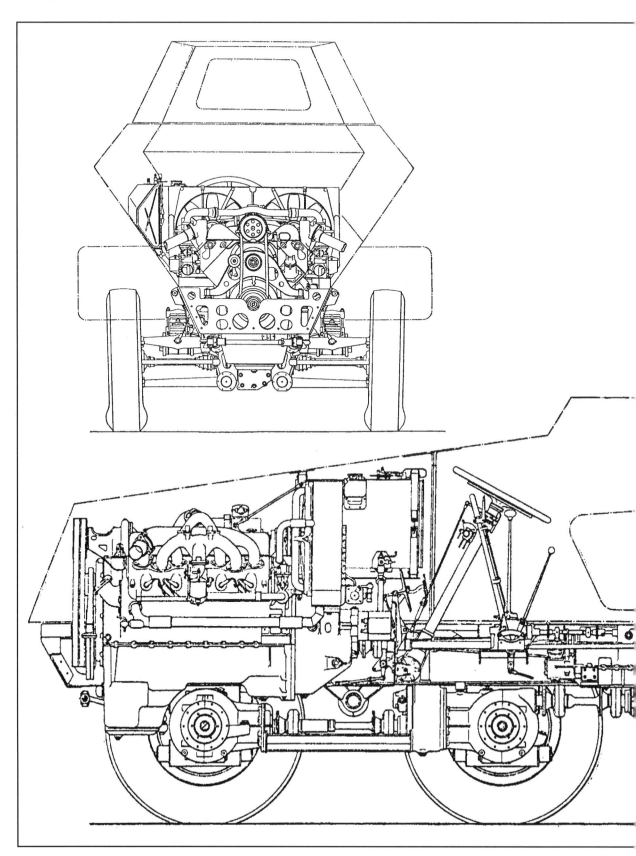

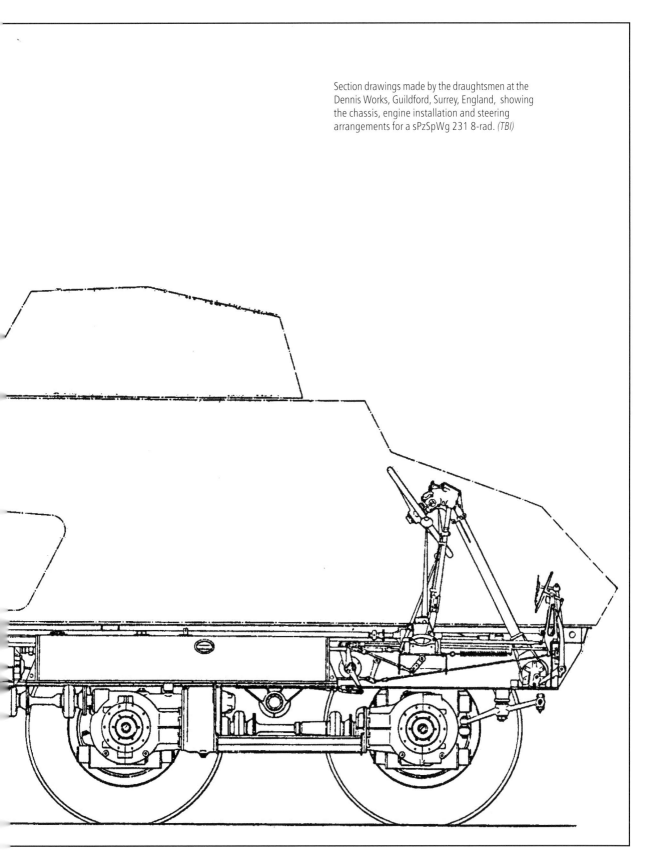

Section drawings made by the draughtsmen at the
Dennis Works, Guildford, Surrey, England, showing
the chassis, engine installation and steering
arrangements for a sPzSpWg 231 8-rad. *(TBI)*

CHAPTER THREE

HULL, TURRET & GUNS

This chapter will deal mainly with the armoured hull, turret and armament of the sPzSpWg SdKfz 231 (8-Rad) as it was the main vehicle in its series, together with the generally similar sPzSpWg (Fu) SdKfz 232 (8-Rad), with the radio installation, which remained in production until 1943.

According to some references, the armoured hull of the *Achtrad* series was supposed to have been greatly influenced by the armour arrangements on some contemporary Czech armoured cars. No solid evidence survives to support this supposition. Generally speaking the armoured plates that together formed the hull (other than the hull floor) all had some degree of slope to deflect incoming fire, thereby enhancing the protection for the interior. The price that had to be paid for this overall protective shape was that it required considerable time, skill and resources to manufacture.

Armoured Hull

The armoured hull was in two main sections. The main, larger section included the forward part of the vehicle, the turret location superstructure and the area just to its rear. The other section covered the engine area from a position roughly in line with the radiator and to the rear. As this arrangement was meant to facilitate access to the engine area, the two sections were bolted together so that the rear

section could be removed when necessary. The engine provided an extra measure of protection by being positioned at the rear of the vehicle.

Both hull sections were of welded construction, using a single layer of flat, surface-hardened armour plates with a Brinell number of 450 to 500. The side plates presented an angle (from the horizontal) of 37°22' with the upper surfaces presenting an angle of -49°10'. Although it was no doubt unintended, the sloping lower hull plates would have served to deflect at least some of the blast effects resultant on a wheel detonating an anti-tank mine, even if the hull floor plates were flat.

The usual access to the left-hand drive position for the front driver was through one of the turret hatches, although there was also an escape hatch located in the front hull top plate. The commander and gunner, both located in the turret, used the same turret access hatches. Access to the rear driver station was via one of two hatches, one in each of the hull sides between the wheel dust covers located over each road wheel pair. These hull hatches could also serve as emergency exits. The wheel cover tops had securing points to which various items of kit or equipment could be strapped or

Above:
The officer of an SdKfz 231 gives instructions to the driver as it fords a river in Yugoslavia. *(BA)*

Left:
An SdKfz 231 passing the Parliament buildings in Athens, 27 April, 1941. *(BA)*

Above:
A captured sPzSpWg SdKfz 231 8-rad in North Africa loaded on a captured Italian Army truck ready to be returned to an Allied base for detailed examination and trials. *(TM)*

lashed, with more similar points located around the hull. Pioneer tools were carried strapped to the front hull.

Numerous vision ports were provided, the two driver stations each having four vision slots, two to the front and one each side. On late production models one of the rear slots was omitted, leaving just the one on the left (when the vehicle was travelling to the rear). All the slots had armoured covers that could be hinged down to the closed position when in action, vision then being through *Schutzgläser* (bullet proof, laminated glass vision blocks) about 2in (50mm) thick. The front driver had a fairly wide field of vision but the length of the rear hull made vision for the rear driver more problematic. For this reason most vehicles were initially supplied with a small mast at each corner to indicate the exact width and extremes of the hull. In practice these masts were soon broken off by day-to-day wear and tear and appear to have been replaced only rarely.

As the vehicles were meant for the reconnaissance role only, the armoured protection was relatively light overall to avoid the excessive weight that would otherwise restrict the vehicle's mobility. The plates were

meant to be able to defeat only conventional rifle bullets, light shell splinters and the lightest anti-tank guns or anti-tank rifles. The vehicles remained vulnerable to anything heavier as the front and sides of the hull were only .32in (8mm) thick, while plates around the engine were 10mm thick. Top hull plates had a depth of only .2in (5mm). From May 1942 onwards, the late production models had the front armour depth increased to 1.2in (30mm), a modification dictated by combat experience and by the fact that Allied anti-armour weapons were becoming increasingly powerful.

One interim protective modification prior to the final increase in hull armour depth was introduced from about early 1940 onwards. To add extra protection over the frontal area, production examples were provided with a frontal stand-off armour plate about .32in (8mm) thick mounted on a bracket. Known as a *Pakschütz*, this extra protection assembly could double as a method of pressing down tall brush and other vegetation through which the vehicle might have to travel. In the field it was also employed as an extra stowage container in which to carry items such as camouflage netting and similar materials. From May 1942 onwards this frontal assembly was deleted after

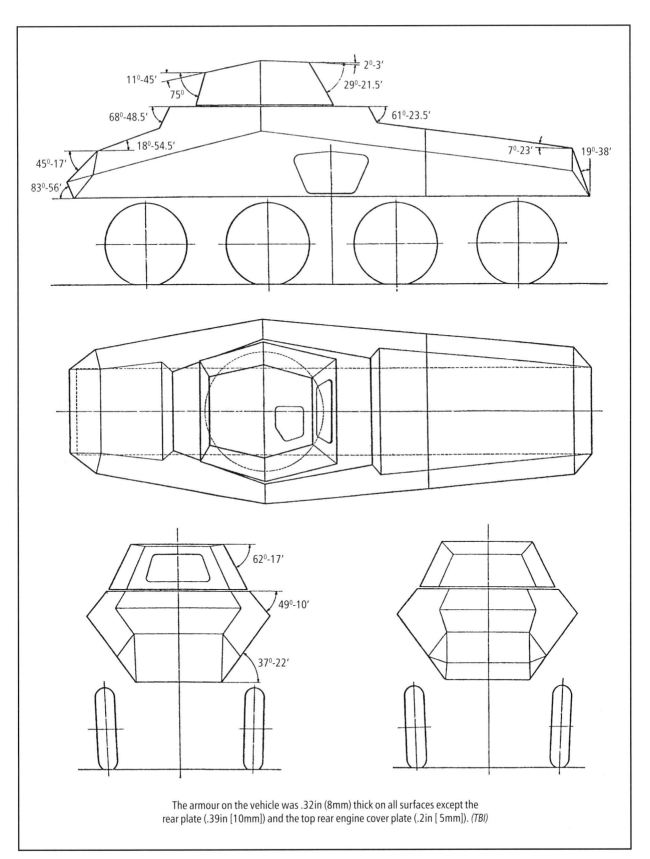

The armour on the vehicle was .32in (8mm) thick on all surfaces except the
rear plate (.39in [10mm]) and the top rear engine cover plate (.2in [5mm]). *(TBI)*

it was decided to increase the frontal armour to a depth of 1.2in (30mm). The *Pakschütz* was therefore no longer needed.

Turret

The 360° traverse *Achtrad* turret housed the commander, seated on the left, with the gunner on the right. Six welded plates made up the turret sides, plus the roof. The turret was manufactured using the same armour plate as for the hull. Armour thicknesses were .32in (8mm) for the sides, .22in (5.5mm) for the roof and .59in (15mm) over the armament mantlet. The side plates were placed at an angle of 62°12' below the horizontal to present projectile deflection surfaces.

Access for both turret occupants was via a roof hatch or two hatches in the turret's rear wall. The armament protruded through a mantlet located in the hull front plate. Inside the hull the interior was relatively spacious for an armoured combat vehicle, partially brought about by the front driver using an inverted steering wheel, so he could be seated further forward, and also by the way the commander and gunner were seated in the turret. Both were seated on a tubular frame that hung down from the turret itself. This arrangement did away with the usual need for a rotating cage traversing over the hull floor and saved considered internal space that could then be used for equipment and crew kit stowage.

The turret rotated on ball bearings and was provided with two separate sets of traversing controls. The commander, after observing the battlefield through a periscope, could operate the high-geared auxiliary control operated by a hand crank. This rapid traverse control was used to quickly turn the turret to face a selected target. Once facing the target the gunner could then operate his more finely geared control system and narrow field of view optical sight to lay the armament on the target in both elevation and traverse – then fire, with firing accomplished by pressing the gunner's foot pedal. The commander could also use his turret traverse controls in conjunction with a

Somewhere in the
Balkans — two
sPzSpWg SdKfz 231
8-rad armoured cars
negotiating a mountain
road with a SdKfz 222
armoured car in the
background. *(TM)*

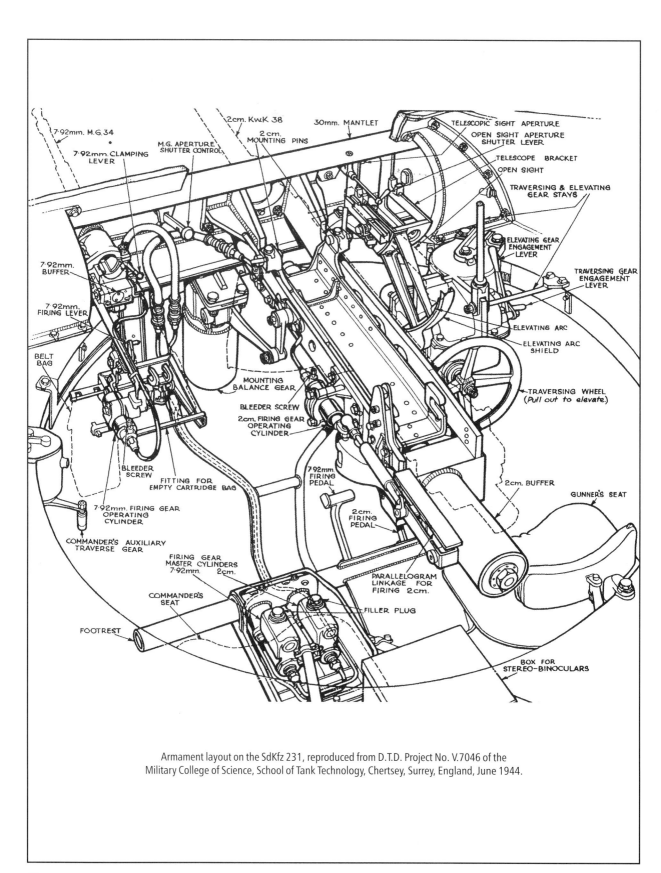

Armament layout on the SdKfz 231, reproduced from D.T.D. Project No. V.7046 of the
Military College of Science, School of Tank Technology, Chertsey, Surrey, England, June 1944.

periscope to which a camera could be attached to provide records of the local terrain or specific areas.

Armament

The main armament of the sPzSpWg SdKfz 231 (8-rad) and the sPzSpWg (Fu) SdKfz 232 (8-rad) was a *2cm KampfwagenKanone 30 L/55* (KwK 30 L/55) cannon mounted co-axially with a *7.92mm Maschinengewehr 34* (MG34) machine gun. The KwK 30 cannon was mounted centrally in a mantlet and was the gunner's main responsibility. The machine gun was mounted to the left of the turret and in front of the commander's position so that he could load or reload the belts when necessary and, on occasion, fire it independently. Barrel elevation for both weapons was from -10° to +26°, while the turret could traverse a full 360°.

The 2cm KwK 30 L/55 was manufactured by Rheinmetall-Borsig AG of Düsseldorf. It was a development of the 20mm Solothurn S5-100 developed by Rheinmetall-Borsig

engineers working away from Versailles Treaty observer scrutiny at Solothurn, Switzerland during the 1920s. The S5-100 was adopted in a slightly modified form by the German armed forces as their standard light anti-aircraft gun from 1935 onwards as the *2cm Fliegerabwehrkanone 30 L/65* (2cm FlaK 30 L/65). The 2cm KwK 30 was a derivative of the FlaK 30, differing mainly in having the barrel length reduced to 55 calibres (about 3.6ft [1.1mtr]), plus some alterations introduced to allow the cannon to be mounted in an armoured vehicle mantlet. The KwK 30 remained recoil-operated and was fed from side-loaded 20-round box magazines inserted into the left of the receiver (looking toward the muzzle).

From 1940 onwards the KwK 30 was joined in service by the 2cm KwK 38 L/55. The two cannon models were used to arm several other light armoured vehicles other than the *Achtrad* series. The KwK 38 was essentially the same gun as before but modified by Mauser-Werke AG at Obendorf-am-Neckar to increase the cyclic fire rate. The KwK 30 had a cyclic fire rate of 280 rounds per minute (rpm), reduced to a practical 120rpm by the need to change

Above:
A disarmed sPzSpWg SdKfz 231 8-rad with the *Pakschütz* position and shape clearly shown. This is another captured example. *(TM)*

Above:
An *SdKfz 231* passing trees felled by the French in an attempt to block a road, May 1940. *(BA)*

magazines at frequent intervals. With the KwK 38 the rates were 420-480 rpm and 180-220 rpm respectively. These rate of fire increases were carried over to the KwK 38 from the 2cm FlaK 38, the latter remaining in large-scale production at several factories until 1945. It is thought that nearly all KwK 38 production was carried out at Mauser-Werke AG.

The increased rate of fire made a considerable difference to the effectiveness of the anti-aircraft weapons but made no practical difference to the gunners on the sPzSpWg SdKfz 231 (8-rad) and sPzSpWg (Fu) SdKfz 232 (8-rad) as they usually fired the cannon on single shot (semi-automatic) only to improve accuracy. Also in practice, the KwK 30 and KwK 38 served inter-changeably until the end

in 1945, the KwK 38 coming to predominate as the war years progressed.

Both cannon models fired the same ammunition as the 2cm FlaK 30 and FlaK 38, although at a reduced muzzle velocity (2,559ft/sec [780m/sec] as opposed to 2,953ft/sec [900m/sec]) due to the shortened barrel. The usual armoured vehicle round was the armour-piercing *2cm Panzergranate* with a solid hardened steel projectile weighing 4.93oz (140grm). It could penetrate .55in (14mm) of armour plate set at an angle of 60° at 547yd (500mtr). An alternative was the *2cm Panzergranate AP40* where the armour penetration was .79in (20mm) of armour plate set at an angle of 60° at 547yd (500mtr). However, AP40 rounds were rarely encountered due to their need for critically scarce tungsten for

with the main 2 cm cannon. The MG34 was another product with its origins in Switzerland during the 1920s, but this time the manufacturer was the Mauser-Werke AG at Obendorf-am-Neckar and its other facilities in Berlin and several other centres. It was developed as a general purpose machine gun (GPMG) for the infantry, which meant it could be fired from either a heavy tripod for the sustained fire ground role, or from a bipod for the lighter, infantry-portable role. The MG34 was also produced for air defence, fortification, naval and vehicle mountings in many forms so it became a general purpose weapon in every respect.

The MG34 fired at a cyclic rate of about 900rpm, with ammunition fed into the gun in 50 or 250-round belts. Also available was also a 75-round saddle drum and 50-round belt drum. The most commonly used feed arrangement for the *Achtrad* series was the 50-round belt as this was relatively easy to handle within the confines of the turret.

The MG34 proved to be an excellent machine gun but it was expensive and time-consuming to manufacture. From 1942 onwards it was gradually supplemented (but never replaced) by the 7.92mm MG42, a more easily produced Mauser-Werke AG weapon with a cyclic fire rate of 1,500rpm. It would be unwise to state that these were never used with the *Achtrad Waffenträger* (eight-wheel-drive weapons carrier) series but most records mention only the MG34, right until the war ended.

The sPzSpWg SdKfz 231 (8-rad) had stowage facilities for boxes containing 2,100 rounds of 7.92mm in pre-prepared belts. For the sPzSpWg (Fu) SdKfz 232 (8-rad) this was reduced to 1,050 rounds to make room for the extra radio set.

Other weaponry carried by the *Achtrad* series was a single 9mm MP38 or MP40 sub-machine gun for close-in vehicle defence or dismounted use by one of the crew. Space for 192 rounds of 9mm ammunition was provided in the hull. The only other weapon-related internal stowage was for a 27mm signal pistol together with its associated cartridges. Some late production models replaced the signal pistol with smoke dischargers intended not for signalling but for rapidly producing smoke screens for concealment. Six *Stielhandgranate* 24 high-explosive/fragmentation stick grenades were also carried.

the sub-calibre penetrators. The KwK 30 and KwK 38 could also fire a small high-explosive projectile (*Sprenggranate*) weighing 4.2oz (119grm), although its limited explosive payload rendered it a largely ineffective round.

The sPzSpWg SdKfz 231 (8-rad) and sPzSpWg (Fu) SdKfz 232 (8-rad) both carried 180 rounds of 2cm ammunition in nine pre-loaded magazines.

The 7.92mm MG34 was exactly the same machine gun as that used by the rest of the German armed forces, other than some slight mounting modifications to allow it to be mounted in an armoured vehicle mantlet. On the sPzSpWg SdKfz 231 (8-rad) and sPzSpWg (Fu) SdKfz 232 (8-rad) mantlet mounting the machine gun elevated and traversed together

CHAPTER FOUR

SdKfz 231 VARIANTS

This chapter will provide the main changes where
individual variants within the SdKfz 231 series
differed from the general outlines described
in the previous pages.

As a general rule the first three models in the series followed the same functions as their equivalents in the 6-rad heavy armoured reconnaissance vehicle series, but with the addition of one further heavily armed variant.

sPzSpWg SdKfz 231 (8-rad)

As this vehicle was used as the basis for the general descriptions provided in the previous sections reference should be made to them for details. One item not previously described was the radio installation, common to all vehicles in the early *Achtrad* series. This was a *FunkSprechGerät 'a'* (FuSprGer 'a'), a radio telephone equipment meant only for inter-vehicle communications and widely employed by all armoured vehicles other than tanks. It employed a 4.6 or 6.6ft (1.4 or 2mtr) high flexible rod aerial enabling an operating range of about .62miles (1km) while on the move or up to 1.7miles (3km) when the vehicle was stationary. If the radio ever failed, recourse then had to be made to the semaphore flags carried on every vehicle.

sPzSpWg (Fu) SdKfz 232 (8-rad)

In general this variant was exactly the same as the sPzSpWg SdKfz 231(8-rad) with the addition of a long-range radio and the associated antennae. The extra radio was the *FunkSprechGerät 12* (FuSprGer 12) operating on the medium wave 1,120 to 3,000Kc/s or 850 to 3,000Kc/s bands. The voice operating range was up to 15.5miles (25km). Using morse signals the range was up to 49.7miles (80km).

Having an 80-Watt transmitter, the FuSprGer 12 originally employed a rather cumbersome tubular frame aerial array with the front of the frame supported by a swivelling post located on the turret roof. As well as being cumbersome and conspicuous the frame array had the disadvantage that its two rear supports could be accidentally shot through when the armament was deployed towards the rear. Improvements in radio technology did away with the frame array on later models, the frame being replaced by a single flexible rod aerial 6.6ft (2mtr) high, with a star array at the top.

Above:
Another view of the sPzSpWg SdKfz 231 8-rad en route to an Allied base for extended examination and tests. *(TM)*

Left:
A sPzSpWg (5 cm) SdKfz 234/2 Puma on the Eastern Front — note the star aerial denoting that this is a command vehicle. *(TM)*

Above:
A good general view of a sPzSpWg (7.5 cm) SdKfz 234/3 showing the bulky size of the main armament, a centrally mounted 7.5 cm KwK 51 L/24. *(TM)*

Reports mention that the FuSprGer 12 proved rather troublesome in service and required constant maintenance and adjustments.

As mentioned elsewhere the 7.92mm ammunition carried by this variant was limited to 1,050 rounds due to the space occupied by the extra radio installation. The main 2cm KwK 30 or KwK 38 cannon armament was retained.

Production figures for the sPzSpWg SdKfz 231 (8-rad) and the sPzSpWg (Fu) SdKfz 232 (8-rad) were usually shown together with no differentiation between the two. The production total for both reached 607 between 1936 and September 1943, although only the sPzSpWg (Fu) SdKfz 232 (8-rad) remained in production after September 1942. Pre-1939 annual production figures have not been found but those for the war years were as follows:

1939	1940	1941	1942	1943
37	26	94	160	200

The two vehicles were expensive. Each vehicle, delivered without weapons, radios or other equipment, cost the German war economy *Reichsmark* (Rm) 52,980. This should be compared to Rm 19,600 for a SdKfz 222, 4 x 4 light armoured reconnaissance vehicle, or Rm 117,00 for a *Panther* tank.

sPzSpWg (Fu) SdKfz 263 (8-rad)

This variant fulfilled the same communication and command centre function as the sPzSpWg (Fu) SdKfz 263 (6-rad). It had a fixed turret superstructure partly formed by the upper hull side plates being extended upwards. This special body was manufacture by the Deutsche Werke at Kiel (most of the armoured hulls for the series were constructed

Above:
Direct overhead illustration of a sPzSpWg (7.5 cm) SdKfz 234/3, showing the 7.5 cm KwK 51 L/24 main armament. (TM)

at Schichau). All other mechanical and hull details were as for the vehicles mentioned above. The only armament was an optional single 7.92mm MG34 machine gun in a ball mounting at the front of the turret superstructure, and a single 9mm MP38 or MP40 sub-machine gun. Stowage was provided for 1,100 rounds of 7.92mm ammunition, plus the usual 192 rounds of 9mm ammunition for the sub-machine gun. The crew number was increased to five, two of them drivers, with the rear driver doubling as a radio operator.

On this variant, the radio installation had the rather imposing name of *FunkSprechGerät für Panzer Funktrupp 'b' (motorisiert)*. This was essentially a long-range equipment capable of communicating with a wide variety of other radios in use in the field. For this vehicle carried a large, rigidly supported, fixed-frame aerial array, larger than that for the SdKfz 232, together with a large star-pattern aerial rod array. On late production examples the frame array was replaced by flexible rod aerials.

Despite being ready for production by the end of 1938, production of this variant did not commence until 1941. During that year only eight were manufactured, with a further 118 during 1942. Production ended in 1943 after a further 40 examples had been added to the overall total.

The cost of this vehicle was even more than the two earlier variants, each example costing Rm 57,290.

sPzSpWg (7.5cm) SdKfz 233

Mentioned here out of numerical sequence, the sPzSpWg (7.5cm) SdKfz 233 had no equivalent in the 6-rad series so the 8-rad suffix could be dropped, only to be replaced by (7.5cm) indicating the calibre of the main armament. Combat experience during the

Right:
A right rear view of a sPzSpWg (7.5 cm) SdKfz 234/3. Note the louvres for cooling air over the engine compartment. The engine cover plate armour was .19in (5mm) thick. *(TM)*

early war year campaigns had indicated that armoured reconnaissance operations would benefit greatly from the introduction of heavy support weapon platforms travelling with the units. It was therefore decided to introduce an entirely new *Achtrad* variant carrying a 75mm close support gun.

The gun involved was the *7.5cm SturmKanone 37 L/24* (StuK 37 L/24), although some references make mention of the *7.5cm KampfwagenKanone 37 L/24* (KwK 37 L/24). This confusion is understandable as both guns were essentially the same. The KwK 37 L/24 was originally intended for fixed installations on the early models of the Panzer IV medium tank (all early versions up to Ausf F2) and the Panzer III Ausf N. The StuK 37 L/24 was exactly the same gun, but intended for limited traverse installations on the early models of the *Sturmgeschütz III* (StuG III) assault gun series (up to and including the Ausf E). Both guns fired the same ammunition and had identical ballistic characteristics.

The L/24 in the designations meant that the barrel was only 24 calibres long, resulting in the commonly applied slang name of *Stummelkanone*, literally Stumpy Gun. Due to the short barrel the muzzle velocity was relatively low and the armour penetration performance was limited. When it first appeared as the main armament of the early Panzer IV series, this electrically fired gun had a considerable impact on the armoured warfare scene by being much larger in calibre than any contemporary tank gun (although that state of affairs did not last long). After 1940 the StuK 37 and KwK 37 were gradually replaced for armoured combat by longer-barrelled, higher velocity guns, but the short-barrelled type remained an effective direct fire support gun. It was therefore retained in production by Krupps to be installed on several other armoured vehicles, other than tanks or assault guns, including the SdKfz 250/8 and SdKfz 251/9 half-track armoured personnel carriers and, starting during 1942, the sPzSpWg 7.5cm SdKfz 233.

Above:
Although it looks authentic this is almost certainly a posed shot of a sPzSpWg (Fu) SdKfz 232 8-rad in North Africa — note the absence of any armament on the vehicle. *(TM)*

Left:
A sPzSpWg (Fu) SdKfz 232 8-rad in an unusual guise as it has special wheel rims to patrol lengths of railway line on the Eastern Front. *(TM)*

Above:
The first of four views of a sPzSpWg (7.5 cm) SdKfz 233, this one providing good detail of the side entry hatches and the spare wheel stowage. *(TM)*

Right:
A sPzSpWg (7.5 cm) SdKfz 233 head-on with a good view of the tool stowage and the off-set 7.5 cm StuK 37 L/24 main armament. *(TM)*

Above:
The off-set arrangement of a 7.5 cm StuK 37 L/24 on a sPzSpWg (7.5 cm) SdKfz 233. The vertical-sliding Hotchkiss-type breech is open to receive a fresh round. Note also the periscopic sight. *(TM)*

Left:
In contrast to the above this is a 7.5 cm KwK 51 L/24 on a sPzSpWg (7.5 cm) SdKfz 234/3. *(TM)*

Greek prisoners pass a
*Leibstandarte SS Adolf
Hitler* SdKfz 232 (Fu) in
1941. *(TM)*

Right:
A good detail view of the wheels and rear exhaust covers on a captured sPzSpWg SdKfz 231 8-rad awaiting the first stages of delivery to an Allied base. *(TM)*

Far right:
North Africa, early 1943, and a sPzSpWg (Fu) SdKfz 232 8-rad en route to a mission. Note the extra water and equipment stowed around the vehicle. *(TM)*

Specifications

Model	SdKfz 231	SdKfz 232	SdKfz 263	SdKfz 233
Crew	Four	Four	Five	Three
Weight in combat	18,298.2lb (8,300kg)	19,400.5lb (8,800kg)	19,135.93lb (8,580kg)	18,915.5lb (8,580kg)
Length	19.2ft (5.85mtr)	19.2ft (5.85mtr)	19.2ft (5.85mtr)	19.2ft (5.85mtr)
Width	7.22ft (2.2mtr)	7.22ft (2.2mtr)	7.22ft (2.2mtr)	7.22ft (2.2mtr)
Height	7.7ft (2.34mtr)	9.5ft (2.9mtr)	9.5ft (2.9mtr)	7.4ft (2.25mtr)
Ground clearance	10.64in (2.70mm)	10.64in (2.70mm)	10.64in (2.70mm)	10.64in (2.70mm)
Wheelbase	13.45ft (4.1mtr)	13.45ft (4.1mtr)	13.45ft (4.1mtr)	13.45ft (4.1mtr)
Track	5.25ft (1.6mtr)	5.25ft (1.6mtr)	5.25ft (1.6mtr)	5.25ft (1.6mtr)
Max speed, road	53mph (86km/h)	53mph (85km/h)	62mph (100km/h)	49.7mph (80km/h)
Max speed, cross country	18.6mph (30km/h)	18.6mph (30km/h)	18.6mph (30km/h)	18.6mph (30km/h)
Fuel capacity	30.5gal (138.5ltr)	30.5gal (138.5ltr)	30.5gal (138.5ltr)	30.5gal (138.5ltr)
Range, road	186.4 miles (300km)	186.4 miles (300km)	186.4 miles (300km)	186.4 miles (300km)
Range, cross country	93.2 miles (150km)	93.2 miles (150km)	93.2 miles (150km)	93.2 miles (150km)
Gradient	30°	30°	30°	30°
Fording	3.28ft (1mtr)	3.28ft (1mtr)	3.28ft (1mtr)	3.28ft (1mtr)
Trench crossing width	4.1ft (1.25mtr)	4.1ft (1.25mtr)	4.1ft (1.25mtr)	4.1ft (1.25mtr)
Vertical obstacle	1.64ft (500mm)	1.64ft (500mm)	1.64ft (500mm)	1.64ft (500mm)

Specifications

Model	SdKfz 231	SdKfz 232	SdKfz 263	SdKfz 233
Engine	7,910cc V-8 Büssing-NAG L8V-GS petrol developing 150 to 155hp at 3,000rpm			
Gearbox	six forward six reverse	six forward six reverse	six forward six reverse	six forward six reverse
Steering	worm and nut	worm and nut	worm and nut	worm and nut
Turning circle	37.4ft (11.4mtr)	37.4ft (11.4mtr)	37.4ft (11.4mtr)	37.4ft (11.4mtr)
Suspension	independent	independent	independent	independent
Tyres	210 x 18	210 x 18	210 x 18	210 x 18
Electrical system	12/24V	12/24V	12/24V	12/24V
Armour				
front	.59in or 1.18in (15 or 30mm)	.59in or 1.18in (15 or 30mm)	.59in or 1.18in (15 or 30mm)	1.18in (30mm) (15 or 30mm)
side	.32in (8mm)	.32in (8mm)	.32in (8mm)	.32in (8mm)
rear	.39in (10mm)	.39in (10mm)	.39in (10mm)	.39in (10mm)
Armament	2cm KwK 30 MG34	2cm KwK 30 MG34	MG34	7.5cm StuK 37 MG42

Above:
US troops helping themselves to a joyride on a captured sPzSpWg (7.5 cm) SdKfz 233, Tunisia, 1943. *(TM)*

Right:
The main 7.5 cm KwK 51 L/24 gun installation on a sPzSpWg (7.5 cm) SdKfz 234/3 — compare this picture with that on page 53 (top). *(TM)*

Far right:
A sPzSpWg (7.5 cm) SdKfz 233 showing its off-set 7.5 cm StuK 37 L/24 main armament. *(TM)*

Above:

Direct overhead view of a sPzSpWg (2cm) SdKfz 234/1 with the open-topped turret traversed to allow the 2 cm KwK 38 cannon to fire to the right rear. *(TM)*

To accommodate the gun the upper hull of the *Achtrad* based on the Büssing-NAG GS chassis was extensively modified. The turret was omitted and the main crew compartment was left entirely open. The gun was mounted in a box-pattern mantlet to the right-hand side of the driver, with part of the upper hull superstructure cut away for the purpose. The gun and mantlet were set in a wide armoured shield .59in (15mm) thick. Barrel elevation was from -10° to +12°, with the barrel traversing up to 12° each side.

Much of the combat compartment space was taken up by the gun, with provision having to be made for the length of recoil, so the crew serving the gun was just two, one of whom, the gunner, also had to act as vehicle commander, while the loader also operated the FuSprGer 'a' inter-vehicle radio. Only one driver, who had to transfer to the rear driving station when necessary, was carried. Late production examples had the superstructure side armour extended upwards to provide the gunners with added protection.

Ammunition stowage was provided for 32 rounds, most of which would have been high-explosive, plus a few smoke rounds. Only a few anti-armour rounds were carried by the SdKfz 233 as it was meant to be operating in the reconnaissance role. If they were carried, the armour-penetrating projectiles were of the hollow charge type fired at a muzzle velocity of 1,476ft/sec (450m/sec). The projectile weighed from 9.7 to 10.6lb (4.4 to 4.8kg) (according to type) and was capable (under ideal conditions) of defeating from 2.76 to 3.94in (70 to 100mm) of armour at combat ranges. The high-explosive projectile weighed 15lb (6.8kg), fired with a muzzle velocity of 1,263ft/sec (385m/sec). When delivered from the SdKfz 233 the high-explosive projectiles were almost always fired against direct line-of-sight targets.

By the time the first production SdKfz 233 appeared during early 1943 the standard *Wehrmacht* machine gun had become the 7.92mm MG42. One of these was carried on each SdKfz 233 for local or air defence on free movement pintle mountings arranged around the main combat compartment. The MG42 could also be employed on a bipod for dismounted purposes and was provided with 1,500 rounds of 7.92mm ammunition. Also carried was the usual 9mm MP38 or MP40 sub-machine gun, together with 192 rounds of ammunition.

Production of the sPzSpWg (7.5 cm) SdKfz 233 commenced during late 1942 using hulls

originally intended for the sPzSpWg (Fu) SdKfz 263 (8-rad). By the end of 1942 the first 22 examples had been manufactured, although none was issued for field service until early 1943. During 1943 a further 100 were manufactured, plus a further 56 during 1944. Production had ceased by the end of that year. So popular and successful did these fire-support vehicles become that a further 10 examples were converted to the sPzSpWg SdKfz 233 (7.5cm) configuration using refurbished, battle-weary sPzSpWg SdKfz 231 (8-rad) or sPzSpWg (Fu) SdKfz 232 (8-rad) hulls and chassis.

ARK Chassis Innovations

The official request that led to the final variants of the war-year *Achtrad* series to enter service was issued as early as August 1940. Good as it was, the *Achtrad* series based on the Büssing-NAG GS chassis displayed some undesirable features that the *Wehrmacht* authorities wanted eliminated.

One undesirable feature was the overall height of the vehicles that rendered their overall silhouette too prominent and that much more difficult to conceal during any military operation, bearing in mind that the reconnaissance task was meant to be carried out undetected. There was also the shortcoming that the engine cooling was inadequate under hot conditions. As campaigning in North Africa was already under consideration as early as 1940, *Tropen (Tp)* – tropical modifications would have to be introduced to cater for the extreme heat and dusty conditions likely to be encountered. Another cause of concern was that the operational range should be extended.

It was also decided that the overall hull and drive train design concepts should be retained as far as possible. The result was that the overall visual appearance of the subsequent vehicles remained much the same as before, even though considerable changes were introduced.

One was that the armoured hull assumed monocoque form, acting as the main load bearing structure. Only a vestigial chassis remained, produced as before by Büssing-NAG and known as the ARK. These measures immediately reduced the overall height while increasing the ground clearance and possible wading depth. The height was reduced still further on the main reconnaissance variant, the sPzSpWg (2cm) SdKfz 234/1. The former enclosed turret was removed and replaced by a low-sided, open-topped turret. These measures

Right:
A fine side view of a
sPzSpWg (2 cm) SdKfz
234/1 with the low
open turret traversed
to the rear.

lowered the overall height to 6.9ft (2.1mtr), significantly lower than the 7.7ft (2.35mtr) of the earlier sPzSpWg SdKfz 231(8-rad).

Another major change was to the main power source. Tatra of Nesseldorf, originally a Czech concern until 1938, was asked to design an air-cooled diesel engine specifically for 'tropical' use. Its first attempts at delivering such an engine proved unsuccessful so instead it offered its 14,825cc V-12 Tatra T 103 air-cooled diesel developing 210hp at 2,250rpm. This engine was used to power the rugged and powerful Tatra T 111 heavy truck, later to become legendary for its ability to continue

working under the toughest conditions. To assist the cooling processes, air intake alterations were introduced to the covers over the engine area. The T 111 engine proved to be entirely satisfactory for the variants in the new *Achtrad* series. This was despite the fact that by the time the new series was first manufactured during 1944 the North African campaigning was over. However, the engines gave sterling service on the Eastern Front and in northwest Europe until the war ended.

The hull outline and general layout of the new vehicles remained much the same as for the earlier series. The front hull armour was

1.18in (30mm) thick from the outset and the hull side armour was increased to .57in (14.5mm) in places (.39in [10mm] at the rear). The glacis plate over the front hull was .67in (17mm) thick.

Few gearbox or other drive train modifications were introduced, although the tyres were changed to the wider profile 270 x 20 type. Knorr pneumatic brakes replaced the earlier cable-operated units. The suspension remained basically unaltered, as did the complicated dual-position steering system. A larger 52.8gal (240ltr) fuel tank was introduced, providing an increase in operational road range to 373 miles (600km). The

tank was afterwards increased in volume to 79gal (360ltr) to provide a further road range increase of up to 621.4 miles (1,000km), or 342.8 miles (550km) off road.

One external visual change was a that a single dust guard assembly each side replaced the earlier two-wheel cover units, providing space for four more stowage compartments each side to accommodate equipment and crew kit.

There was also a change of production venue. *Achtrad* with the ARK chassis were completed at the Büssing-NAG facility at Leipzig. The armoured hulls continued to the manufactured by the Deutsche Edelstahlwerke at Krefeld.

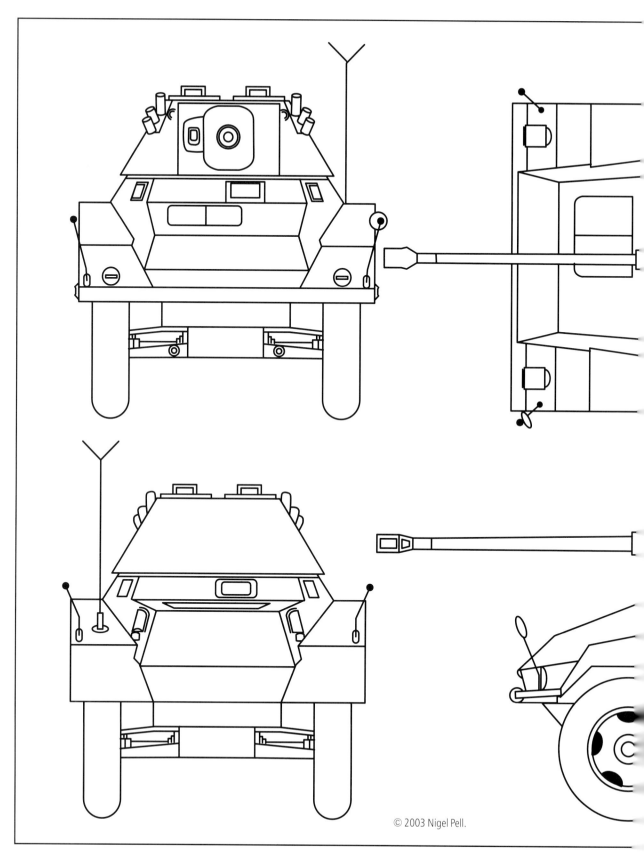

© 2003 Nigel Pell.

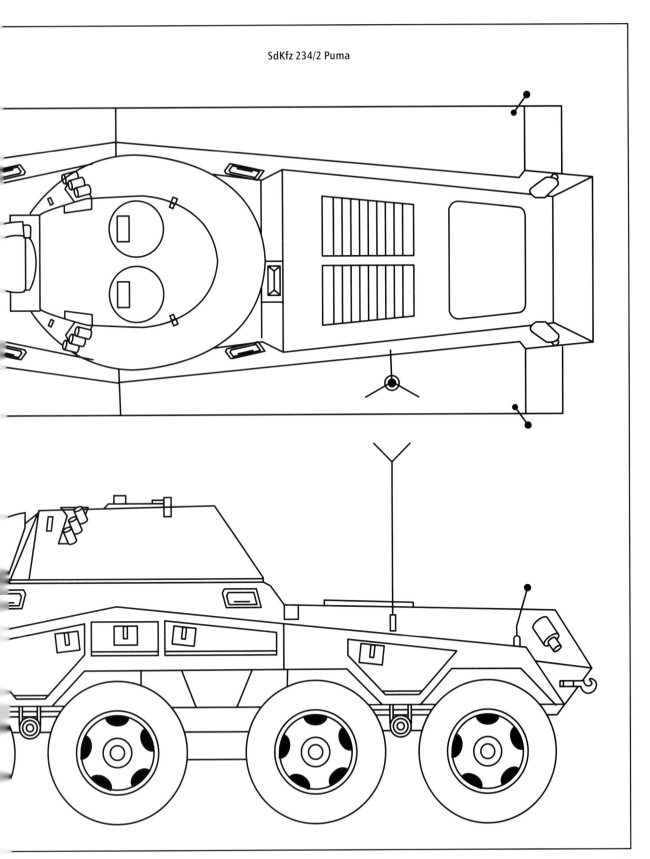

SdKfz 234/2 Puma

CHAPTER FIVE

SdKfz 234 VARIANTS

The SdKfz 234 was the final model of the 8-rad series
and was produced in larger numbers than any other model.
Its role was that of heavy armoured reconnaissance
mounting guns from 2cm to 7.5cm bore.

This variant was produced in larger numbers than any other of the SdKfz 234 series as it was the main heavy armoured reconnaissance version.

sPzSpWg (2cm) SdKfz 234/1

The main-armament guns were mounted in a low-sided, fully-rotating, open-topped turret made up from six flat armoured plates, 1.18in (30mm) thick at the front and .32in (8mm) thick at the sides and rear. The SdKfz 234/1 crew remained as before: commander, gunner and two drivers.

The turret involved was known as a *2cm Hänglafette 38* (Swinging Mount 38). A generally similar turret was already in use on the SdKfz 222 armoured car and the SdKfz 250/9 light half-track, both vehicles serving in the light armoured reconnaissance role. The same turret was also a feature of the fully-tracked *Aufklärer auf Fahrgestell Panzerkraftwagen 38(t)*, the only tracked reconnaissance vehicle still in production when the war ended.

The decision to leave the turret open was taken mainly to improve the crew's all-round vision. Combat experience demonstrated it was vulnerable to the ingress of hand grenades delivered by infantry tank-killer squads. The open top was therefore covered by a stiff wire mesh cover that could hinge open along the centre (fore and aft) when necessary. The armament was as before, a single 2cm KwK 38 L/55 cannon, with a single co-axial machine gun mounted to the left, this time a 7.92mm MG42. The armament firing slots were open at the top to allow both weapons to be elevated up to +70° for air defence. The minimum elevation angle was 0°. One innovation was that the gunner could fire both weapons using levers on the traversing wheels to actuate Bowden cables connected to the trigger mechanisms.

Ammunition stowage was increased compared to the earlier *Achtrad* models. Stowage was provided along the left-hand side of the combat compartment for 480 rounds in 20 pre-loaded box magazines. 2,400 rounds of 7.92mm ammunition were carried in 50-round belts inside ammunition boxes. As usual, a single 9mm MP38 or MP 40 sub-machine was standard, along with the usual allotment of 192 rounds.

Above:
The well preserved sPzSpWg (7.5 cm lang) SdKfz 234/4 held by the Panzer Museum, Germany. *(RG/TM)*

Left:
A frontal view of the Panzer Museum's sPzSpWg (7.5 cm lang) SdKfz 234/4 showing the 7.5 cm PaK 40 barrel held in the travelling clamp. *(RG/TM)*

Above:
The breech of the 7.5 cm PaK 40 anti-tank gun carried as the main armament of the sPzSpWg (7.5 cm lang) SdKfz 234/4. *(RG/TM)*

Right:
This view of the main armament of the sPzSpWg (7.5 cm lang) SdKfz 234/4 clearly shows the gunner's controls and the location of the direct vision optical sight (not installed). *(RG/TM)*

Above:
Looking down and to the rear of the breech of the 7.5 cm PaK 40 gun installation in the sPzSpWg (7.5 cm lang) SdKfz 234/4. Note the steering wheel at the rear driving position. *(RG/TM)*

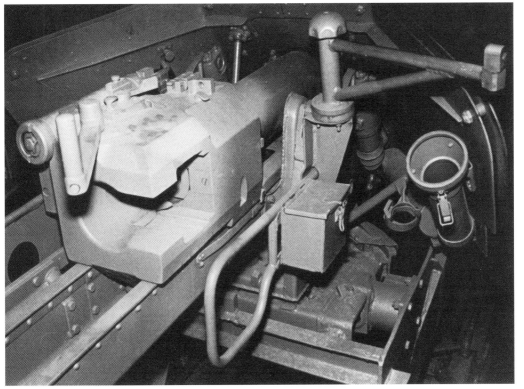

Left:
The right-hand area of the 7.5 cm Pak 40 gun of the sPzSpWg (7.5 cm lang) SdKfz 234/4 — the arm to the right was provided to mount a 7.92 mm machine gun. *(RG/TM)*

The radio installation for the SdKfz 234/1 was the same as that for the earlier SdKfz 232 (8-Rad), although frame aerials were never involved, only flexible rod aerials. It therefore consisted of a *FunkSprechGerät 'a'* (FuSprGer 'a') inter-vehicle radio telephone, and a FuSprGer 12, allowing each vehicle to act as its own communication centre.

Considering that the first diesel-engined example was ready during 1942 it took some time for series production of the SdKfz 234/1 to commence - not until June 1944. From September 1943 onwards it was decreed that at least half of all SdKfz 234 series production would be devoted to the SdKfz 234/1 variant. This was later increased to 75% but such dictates were by then largely academic. By the time production commenced the German industrial and transport infrastructure was crumbling under Allied bombing attacks. Despite being awarded a high production priority, only 163 examples had been manufactured by the end of 1944, plus a further 37 before production was terminated at the end of January 1945.

sPzSpWg (5cm) SdKfz 234/2 Puma

As early as 1938 German intelligence agencies had noted that the Soviet Army was already fielding T-26 light tanks armed with 45mm main guns for the armoured reconnaissance role. One possible counter for this situation was for the Germans to develop a matching vehicle, but armed with a 5cm gun. An order was therefore placed for such a vehicle during August 1939, although subsequent development was unhurried. The vehicle emerged as the *Panzerkraftwagen II Ausf L SdKfz 123 Luchs* (Lynx). The first 100 of these light reconnaissance tanks completed were armed with a single 2cm KwK 38 cannon, the intention being that subsequent production would involve a version, known as the Leopard, having a turret mounting the 5cm KwK 39/1 L/60, high-velocity gun. Daimler-Benz designed and developed the turret, commencing turret production well before the Leopard was supposed to enter production. It never did. In January 1943 an order dictated that, due to its high cost in resources and raw materials, all further work relating to the SdKfz 123 Lynx/Leopard would cease.

One further reason why the Lynx/Leopard was terminated was that an alternative had been proposed. This placed the Leopard 5cm gun turret on the SdKfz 234 series hull, creating a powerful, heavy armoured reconnaissance vehicle well capable of defending itself against Soviet equivalents. It took relatively little work to adapt the hull top to carry the two-man

turret so series production could commence during September 1943, some months before the first sPzSpWg (2 cm) SdKfz 234/1. The new vehicle became the sPzSpWg (5cm) SdKfz 234/2 Puma. The crew remained as before: commander, gunner and two drivers.

The oval-contoured turret had sloping sides which greatly assisted incoming shot deflection. The main gun, the high-velocity 5cm KwK 39/1 L/60, was ballistically identical to the towed 5cm PaK 38 anti-tank gun, both using the same muzzle-braked 60-calibre barrel and firing the same ammunition. The gun had a vertical, semi-automatic breech mechanism and was balanced in its mounting by a spring-type equilibriator between the gun cradle and turret roof. The recoil mechanism was housed within the protection afforded by the mantlet. Both the gun and a 7.92mm MG42 machine gun were mounted co-axially in a *Saukopf* (Pig's head) cast mantlet up to 3.94in (100mm) thick at its deepest point. This added considerably to

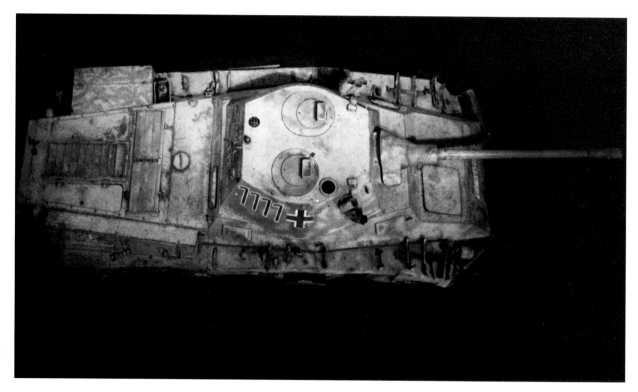

Above:
An overhead view
taken from an
Allied technical report
and showing good
detail of a sPzSpWg
(5 cm) SdKfz 234/2
Puma. *(TM)*

Right:
Frontal view of a
sPzSpWg (5 cm) SdKfz
234/2 Puma taken
from the same
technical report. *(TM)*

the protection provided by the 1.18in (30mm) thick turret front plate; the turret sides were .57in (14.5mm) thick. One further protective measure was a bank of three screening smoke grenade launchers either side of the turret front.

The gun fired a solid projectile weighing 4.54lb (2.06kg) with a muzzle velocity of 2,700ft/sec (823m/sec). Electrically-fired, it could defeat 2.17in (55mm) of armour at 2,734yd (250mtr). Fifty-five rounds of 5cm ammunition were carried along with 2,850 rounds of 7.92mm ammunition for the MG42. The usual 9mm MP38 or MP40 was not forgotten and neither were the normal 192 rounds of 9mm ammunition.

When the Puma was ordered into production a total of 500 was requested, with output commencing during September 1943. This was later increased to 1,000 but such targets became increasingly unlikely as the war continued. When production ceased in September 1944 the final production total was 101, seven by the end of 1943 and the remaining 94 during 1944.

The Puma hull and turret combination proved to be remarkably successful and had a considerable impact on similar armoured car design, not only during the war years but after.

sPzSpWg (7.5cm kurz) SdKfz 234/3

The sPzSpWg (7.5cm kurz) SdKfz 234/3 carried out exactly the same combat functions as the earlier sPzSpWg (7.5cm) SdKfz 233, mounting a 7.5cm gun in an open-topped SdKfz 234 series hull. The crew remained four, two drivers and two gunners, one of whom also acted as vehicle commander.

The gun, still 24 calibres long, differed only slightly from the original 7.5cm StuK 37, the main differences being confined to simplified manufacturing procedures. A new designation was therefore applied, this time *7.5cm Kanone 51 L/24* (7.5cm K 51 L/24). There was also a 7.5cm K 51/1 L/24 with differences too small to notice. The gun mounting differed from the original by being high enough to protrude over the upper front plate, rather than being set into it. The gun shield and mantlet remained much the same as before. Traverse remained 12° either side, with elevation from -3° to +12°. The high explosive projectile, the main type of projectile carried, weighed 15lb (6.8kg), and was fired at a muzzle velocity of 1,263ft/sec

Above:
Front and top turret detail for the sPzSpWg (5 cm) SdKfz 234/2 Puma. *(TM)*

The gunner's sights
and controls for the
main 5 cm gun
armament of the
sPzSpWg (5 cm) SdKfz
234/2 Puma. The
main telescopic sight
is not fitted although
the pillar to the right of
the sight installation is
one of the balancing
equilibriators for the
gun. *(TM)*

(385m/sec). Only a few of the 50 rounds carried had armour piercing, shaped charge warheads.

Other armament used with this variant included an optional bipod-mounted 7.92mm MG42 machine gun for local defence with 1,950 rounds. There was no formal mounting for this machine gun on the vehicle, although it appears that some crews devised various forms of air defence mounting. Also carried was the usual 9mm MP38 or MP40 sub-machine gun with 192 rounds of 9mm of ammunition.

Specifications

Model	SdKfz 234/1	SdKfz 234/2	SdKfz 234/3	SdKfz 234/4
Crew	Four	Four	Five	Three
Weight in combat	25,352.9lb (11,500kg)	25,882lb (11,740kg)	25,352.9lb (11,500kg)	25,352.9lb (11,500kg)
Length	19ft (5.8mtr)	2.3ft (6.8mtr [inc gun])	19.27ft (5.86mtr)	19.7ft (6mtr)
Width	7.64ft (2.33mtr)	7.64ft (2.33mtr)	7.64ft (2.33mtr)	7.64ft (2.33mtr)
Height	6.9ft (2.1mtr)	7.8ft (2.38mtr)	7.25ft (2.21mtr)	7.25ft (2.21mtr)
Ground clearance	1.15ft (350mm)	1.15ft (350mm)	1.15ft (350mm)	1.15ft (350mm)
Wheelbase	13.12ft (4.mtr)	13.12ft (4.mtr)	13.12ft (4.mtr)	13.12ft (4.mtr)
Track	6.39ft (1.95mtr)	6.39ft (1.95mtr)	6.39ft (1.95mtr)	6.39ft (1.95mtr)
Max speed, road	56mph (90km/h)	56mph (90km/h)	56mph (90km/h)	56mph (90km/h)
Max speed, cross country	18.6mph (30km/h)	18.6mph (30km/h)	18.6mph (30km/h)	18.6mph (30km/h)
Fuel capacity	79gal (360ltr)	79gal (360ltr)	79gal (360ltr)	79gal (360ltr)
Range, road	621.4 miles (1,000km)	621.4 miles (1,000km)	621.4 miles (1,000km)	621.4 miles (1,000km)
Range, cross country	342.8 miles (550km)	342.8 miles (550km)	342.8 miles (550km)	342.8 miles (550km)
Gradient	30°	30°	30°	30°
Fording	3.94ft (1.2mtr)	3.94ft (1.2mtr)	3.94ft (1.2mtr)	3.94ft (1.2mtr)
Trench crossing width	4.43ft (1.35mtr)	4.43ft (1.35mtr)	4.43ft (1.35mtr)	4.43ft (1.35mtr)

Right:
North African days, with a sPzSpWg SdKfz 231 8-rad passing a Kfz 15 Wanderer/Horch (divisions of Auto-Union) staff car. *(TG)*

Specifications

Model	SdKfz 231	SdKfz 232	SdKfz 263	SdKfz 233
Vertical obstacle	1.64ft (500mm)	1.64ft (500mm)	1.64ft (500mm)	1.64ft (500mm)
Engine	14,825cc V-12 Tatra T 103 air-cooled diesel developing 210hp at 2,250rpm			
Gearbox	six forward six reverse	six forward six reverse	six forward six reverse	six forward six reverse
Steering	worm and nut	worm and nut	worm and nut	worm and nut
Turning circle	37.4ft (11.4mtr)	37.4ft (11.4mtr)	37.4ft (11.4mtr)	37.4ft (11.4mtr)
Suspension	independent	independent	independent	independent
Tyres	270 x 20	270 x 20	270 x 20	270 x 20
Electrical system	12/24V	12/24V	12/24V	12/24V
Armour				
front	1.18in (30mm)	1.18in (30mm)	1.18in (30mm)	1.18in (30mm)
side	.32in (8mm)	.32in (8mm)	.32in (8mm)	.32in (8mm)
rear	.39in (10mm)	.39in (10mm)	.39in (10mm)	.39in (10mm)
Armament	2cm KwK 30 MG42	5cm KwK 30 39/1 MG42	7.5cm K 51 MG42	7.5cm PaK 40 MG42

Left:
The off-set 7.5 cm main gun denotes that this is a sPzSpWg (7.5 cm) SdKfz 233. Note the external stowage. *(TM)*

Above:
One of the Allied 8 x 8 armoured cars inspired by the *Achtrad* series, this is the South African-built Marmon-Herrington Mk 6 armed with a 2-pounder main gun. Production delays meant that it was never produced in quantity. *(TM)*

Right:
Another view of the Marmon-Herrington Mk 6, this time a late development vehicle with a 6-pounder gun main armament in an enlarged turret. *(TM)*

Above:
An American-produced T18E2 Boarhound, developed in the US to meet a British specification for a desert warfare armoured car and armed with a 6-pounder main gun. The project was later cancelled. *(TM)*

Left:
The Boarhound featured a large cast turret. Note the rear-mounted fuel drums. *(TM)*

Only 88 examples of this variant were manufactured, all between June and December 1944.

sPzSpWg (7.5cm lang) SdKfz 234/4

By 1944 Soviet armour was becoming so predominant over German armoured forces, both in quality and numbers, that reconnaissance units found life increasingly difficult. Calls were raised for defensive measures more powerful than the weapons they were then using. According to some references, the immediate solution was suggested by Hitler himself. This involved placing a 7.5cm anti-tank gun within the same hull arrangements as the sPzSpWg (7.5cm kurz) SdKfz 234/3. The difference in gun armament was denoted by the *lang* (long) suffix as opposed to *kurz* (short), so the new designation became sPzSpWg (7.5cm lang) SdKfz 234/4.

The gun was a 46-calibre 7.5cm PaK 40 L/46 with the trail legs and wheels removed to place the result on the pivot mounting originally occupied by the 7.5cm K51. By 1940 the 7.5cm PaK 40 was the standard *Wehrmacht* anti-tank gun, manufactured in huge numbers as a towed gun or for a variety of self-propelled platforms. It had been introduced to counter the ever-increasing armoured carapaces being applied to Allied tanks, supplementing, but never completely replacing, the lighter 5cm PaK 38. The main armour-piercing projectile fired was the *Panzergranate 40* weighing 9.04lb (4.1kg). The solid projectile could penetrate 6.07in (154mm) of armour at 574yd (500mtr), the muzzle velocity being 3051ft/sec (930m/sec). A high explosive projectile weighing 12.7lb (5.74kg) was a useful alternative against non-armoured targets.

Placing the 7.5 cm PaK 40 L/60 on the SdKfz 234/4 really took the vehicle out of the heavy reconnaissance category and converted it into a *Panzerjäger*, literally tank hunter, since it would have been as effective in the tank-killing role as many of the other *Panzerjäger* then in service. However, the primary combat role for the vehicle was the protection of other reconnaissance vehicles. Reconnaissance troops referred to the vehicle as their *PaK-Wagen* (anti-tank vehicle). Barrel traverse remained

12° either side, as with the short 75mm gun. Maximum barrel elevation was increased to +22°. Due to the length of the fixed rounds, internal ammunition stowage was limited to 12 rounds, a total that must have been too low for tactical comfort. Other weapons were an optional 7.92mm MG42 (1,950 rounds) and the usual 9mm MP38 or MP40 (192 rounds).

The SdKfz 234/4 was the last of the series to enter production, in December 1944. Twenty-five were completed by the end of that month, plus a further 73 from January to March 1945. Production then ceased, even though plans were being prepared to substitute the 7.5cm

PaK 40 by the closely related tank gun model, the 7.5cm KwK 40, also known under a revised designation system as the 7B84.

Postscript

The German *Achträder* had a profound effect on Allied armoured car design and development during the war years. One obvious 'look-alike' emerged with the South African-manufactured Marmon-Harrington Mk 6, an 8 x 8 with similarities to the German original. Another

war vehicle greatly influenced by the *Achtrad* was the T18E2 Boarhound, built in the US to British specifications and mounted a 6-pounder (57mm) gun.

Several other projects could be quoted but the most significant long-term result did not appear until the late 1960s with the appearance of the (then) West German *Luchs* (Lynx) amphibious reconnaissance vehicle. This large 8 x 8, still in service, may not have many visual connections with its war-year counterparts but the design genesis remains the same, even down to the retention of a 20mm cannon as the main armament.

Above:
The German *Luchs* (Lynx) amphibious reconnaissance vehicle developed during the late 1960s and based around the same specifications as the original *Achtrad*. (CFF)

81

Above:
A museum standard example of a sPzSpWg (7.5 cm lang) SdKfz 234/4. *(RG/TM)*

Right:
The breech of the 7.5 cm Stuk 51 L/24 on a sPzSpWg (7.5 cm) SdKfz 234/3. *((RG/TM)*

Above:
The Tank Museum Bovington's example of a sPzSpWg (7.5 cm) SdKfz 234/3 in desert colours. *(RG/TM)*

Left:
The rear driving position of an *Achtrad*, without the driver's seat — note the hatch to the left of the steering wheel. *(RG/TM)*

CHAPTER SIX

OPERATIONS & MARKINGS

The majority of *Achträder* supplied to armoured reconnaissance battalions were usually delivered painted in standard grey or desert yellow. Division and regiment markings were applied on delivery to their units.

On paper, the personnel strength of an Armoured Reconnaissance Battalion was 27 officers, 223 NCOs and 692 unranked soldiers. The battalion came directly under the control of a Panzer Division headquarters and rarely, if ever, deployed as a complete battalion, its assets being assigned to other formations within the division as the Panzer Division commander considered appropriate.

Reconnaissance Battalion

Each battalion was commanded by a head-quarters unit with its own headquarters company and armoured car company equipped with SdKfz 222 light armoured reconnaissance vehicles. There were three further companies, one equipped with Achtrad heavy reconnaissance vehicles and one with SdKfz 222. Both these companies had fire support provided by two half-track or truck-mounted 81mm mortars. The third company was equipped with the Achtrad heavy support weapon platforms and six truck-mounted 81mm mortars. There was also a support company.

Again on paper, the complete battalion, including the support company had 199 vehicles and 22 motor cycles. Of the vehicle total, 124 were armoured.

Balkenkreuz

The *Balkenkreuz* (Balkan Cross) was the national symbol eventually carried by almost every German World War Two military vehicle, although there was considerable variation and modification. For the invasion of Poland the *Ober Kommando der Wehrmacht* (OKW) - the German Armed Forces High Command - ordered that all AFVs should be marked in a prominent position with a solid white cross, approximately 8in (20cm) high, on the hull and turret sides and rear. However, the troops found this far too conspicuous - making them easier targets for enemy gunners - and so they partially or sometimes even completely covered these crosses with mud. Later either dark yellow or black paint supplied for other markings was used to paint out the centre of the cross more completely.

Above:
A sPzSpWg (Fu)
SdKfz 232 8-rad
moving up into
action, precise
location unknown.
Note the prominent
armoured car
battalion symbol
marking on the
front. *(TM)*

Left:
A *Waffen SS* sPzSpWg
(Fu) SdKfz 232 8-rad,
note the all white
Balkenkreuz. *(TM)*

National Insignia 1942-1945 (Standard centre, variants left and right)

Poland, 1939

Poland
(low visibility variant)

Poland
(variant)

1940-1942, Standard

1940-1945, Variant

1943-1945, Variant

North Africa, Variant

1940-1945, Variant

Turret Numbers, colour and outline variations

Afrika Korps insignia variants

Tactical Signs 1935-42

Motorised Reconnaissance
Company

Indep.Recon.
Battalion HQ

Armoured Car
Company

Reconnaissance
Company

HQ Recon. Battalion
Armoured Inf. Regt.

Radio Company

Telephone
Company

Tactical Signs 1943-45

Armoured Car
Company

Light Reconnaissance
Company

Medium Reconnaissance
Company

Heavy Reconnaissance
Company

Motorcycle Platoon

Armoured Radio
Company

Armoured Telephone
Company

After the Polish campaign the lessons learned led to the development of the stencilled silhouette *Balkenkreuz*, which in time with the expansion of conflict to other fronts, had its own four main regional variants. These consisted of a white silhouette cross edged in black to various degrees, the centre either reflecting the vehicle's original colour or overpainted with another colour, usually either black or white, the ends of the cross being usually left open. It was basically similar in proportion to that of the cross in the centre of the *Luftwaffe* insignia, being essentially a silhouette of the original solid cross. In Europe initially most AFVs were *Wehrmacht* grey and the white *Balkenkreuz* was black centred and black-outlined. In North Africa most vehicles were painted either in dark yellow or salmon sand colours, sometimes oversprayed with darker spots or short wavy lines with the *Balkenkreuz* in solid white or in white outline. In Russia vehicles were snow camouflaged in winter with varying degrees of professionalism according to time and supply. Here the *Balkenkreuz* could be outlined in black, completely black or painted in white onto a black field. Later still in Europe as the Allies closed in there was a bewildering array of paints/camouflage used and usually one of the four main *Balkenkreuz* variants.

The state of air cover also influenced circumstances. When there was a danger of friendly fire the engine decks were often draped with the *Swastika* flag – black in a white circle on

a red background. Also broad white recognition bands or rectangles were used. All soon vanished after air supremacy was lost.

All divisions and regiments had their own emblem, whether or not it was displayed on the battlefield. They were used to identify vehicles but were also an important factor in the bonding of each particular unit. They later took the form of individual pictorial designs, often (like the later tank names) of large predators, but encompassing a wide spectrum of other elements including heraldry, local provinces of origin and specific campaigns. However, up until 1941, the actual battlefield divisional signs were closely monitored by the High Command, and there was a rule that Panzer divisions should carry simple geometrical designs or runic symbols as their combat identification. Their success was confirmed in the Polish campaign where they helped deny the enemy knowledge of the formations encountered. Their officially designated colour was yellow but white eventually became more usual.

By 1940 the envisioned ten Panzer divisions were complete, almost all with new signs. After this a division's sign only changed when it was destroyed (or disgraced), until the doubling of the *Panzerwaffe* necessitated even more symbols. Despite the later additional divisional pictorial emblems this geometric/runic marking remained the essential battlefield divisional sign.

Below:
As the only armament carried in the fixed turret of this Achtrad is a 7.92 mm machine gun it means that this is a *Panzerfunkwagen* SdKfz 263 (Fu), a signals vehicle. *(TM)*

Below: As the only armament carried in the fixed turret of this Achtrad is a 7.92 mm machine gun it means that this is a *Panzerfunkwagen* SdKfz 263 (Fu), a signals vehicle. *(TM)*

Panzer Division signs, 1939-1945

Panzer Division signs, 1939-1945

1939   1940   1941-45   1940   1943

9th Panzer Division   10th Panzer Division

1939-45   1941-45   1939-45   1941-45

11th Panzer Division   12th Panzer Division   13th Panzer Division

1941-45   1940-43   1943-45   1941-45   1941-45   1941-45

14th Panzer Division   15th Panzer Division   16th Panzer Division   16th Panzer Division   17th Panzer Division
       1940-43 painted in red, white or black   (Variant)

1941-45   1941-45   1941-45   1941-45   1943-45   1941-45

18th Panzer Division   19th Panzer Division   20th Panzer Division   21st Panzer Division

1941-43   1941   1941-45   1941-45(V)

22nd Panzer Division   23rd Panzer Division   24th Panzer Division

1943-45   1943-45   1943-45   1944   1943-45

25th Panzer Division   26th Panzer Division   27th Panzer Division   116th Panzer Division   Panzer-Lehr Division

Above:
A sPzSpWg SdKfz 231
8-rad in an unusual
green random-
striped camouflage
finish. *(IWM)*

Right:
Note the 60th Panzer
Grenadier Division
on the front of
this sPzSpWg (Fu)
SdKfz 232 8-rad. *(TM)*

Above:
The turret numbering on this sPzSpWg 234/2 Puma is white outlined red. Two of the digits are painted on the front near-side stowage bin (see left). *(TM)*

Left:
This sPzSpWg SdKfz 231 8-rad was part of the 7th Panzer Division operating during the occupation of Southern France during 1942. *(TM)*

Panzer Grenadier Divisions

Grossdeutschland

3rd Panzer Regiment

4th Panzer Regiment

Brandenburg

Führer-Grenadier Batt.

Kurmark

3rd Panzer Grenadier Div.

10th Panzer Grenadier Div.
to 1943

10th Panzer Grenadier Div.
1943-1945

14th Panzer Grenadier Div.

18th Panzer Grenadier Div.

20th Panzer Grenadier Div.

20th Panzer Grenadier Div.
(variant)

22nd (Luftlande)
Panzer Grenadier Div.

25th Panzer Grenadier Div.

60th Panzer Grenadier Div.

60th Panzer Grenadier Div.
(variant)

90th Panzer Grenadier Div.
(variant)

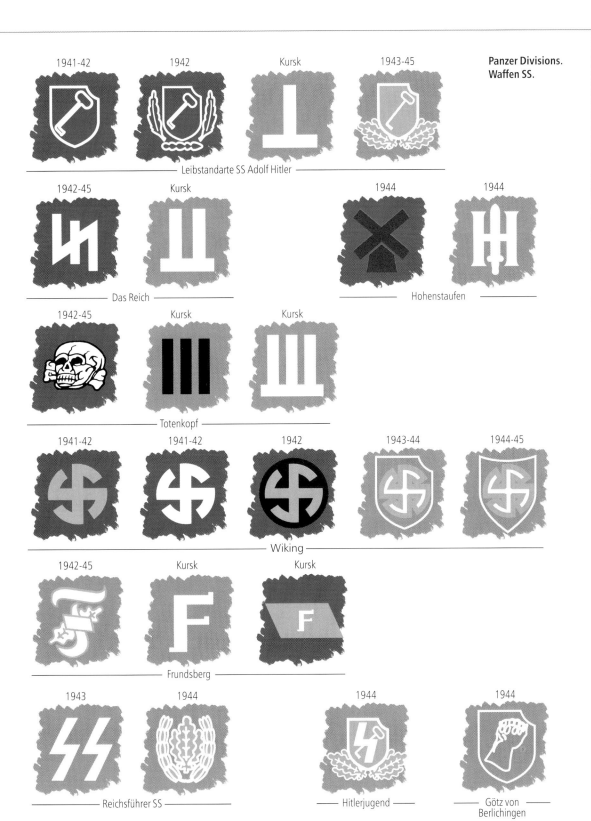

1941-42   1942   Kursk   1943-45

Leibstandarte SS Adolf Hitler

1942-45   Kursk   1944   1944

Das Reich

Hohenstaufen

1942-45   Kursk   Kursk

Totenkopf

1941-42   1941-42   1942   1943-44   1944-45

Wiking

1942-45   Kursk   Kursk

Frundsberg

1943   1944   1944   1944

Reichsführer SS   Hitlerjugend   Götz von Berlichingen

Above: Fine details of the turret area on a sPzSpWg (Fu) SdKfz 232 8-rad. *(TM)*